Advance Praise for
Lessons From the Least of These

"I was brought to the work of urban community development through the teachings and philosophies of Bob Woodson. Those familiar with Mr. Woodson's lifelong work know that his legacy is best reflected in those he personally touches and the countless others he will influence with his Woodson Principles. Within the urban gardens of America, people like Bob Woodson have planted a family tree that sprouts the leaves of shared knowledge, experiences, and relationships that foster a common bond between friends and strangers alike."

—Jamie Elder, Stand Together

"Bob Woodson's book debunks the utopian fantasies of people who presume to know what the poor need, using the wisdom and words of the poor themselves. I hope people listen to him, and more importantly, listen to the people who have been victimized for generations by terrible public policy."

—Mark Levin, Author, Radio and TV Broadcaster

"Bob is on the path to becoming an enjoyable Upton Sinclair—the Sinclair we always needed. He proves that with *Lessons From the Least of These: The Woodson Principles*. He exposes wrongdoing, humanely and without 'gotcha' tactics. He gives voice to the voiceless. He tells their stories. Give it a read—it's enthralling."

—Glenn Beck, Radio Hall of Fame Inductee
and Bestselling Author

"Bob Woodson does not offer theory or speculation. He speaks from decades in the trenches, supporting self-help efforts to improve the quality of life for poor people—working from the bottom up, not the top down. The lessons are profound and instructive."

—Bernard E. Anderson, Ph.D., The Wharton
School, University of Pennsylvania

"After covering Bob Woodson's award-winning work for more than thirty years, this is the book that I long have hoped he would write. In troubled communities where way too much bad news has happened, Woodson has helped local residents to come together, grow effective leaders, and turn the bad news good. Along the way, he also has learned valuable, thought-provoking life lessons like those he has gathered in this book. The result is a valuable gift that appeals across partisan or sectarian lines in the pragmatic, problem-solving spirit he expressed to me years ago: It's not what's 'right' or 'left' that counts, but 'what works'."

—Clarence Page, syndicated *Chicago Tribune* columnist,
winner of the Pulitzer Prize for commentary in 1989

"Bob Woodson is the one leader on the issue of poverty that every American should know. The insights in his book come from decades of experience with real people in real communities, and the rest of us couldn't do better than to listen to what he says."

—Eric Metaxas, #1 *New York Times* bestselling author and
host of the nationally syndicated *Eric Metaxas Radio Show*

"Bob Woodson's *Lessons from the Least of These* offers a powerful remedy for the perennial problems plaguing black communities. Woodson is the man of the hour because he holds the key to liberating both white and black Americans from the failed policies and ideologies that have kept both groups in a vicious cycle of co-dependency. Woodson is a visionary with a plan for saving the most vulnerable in our communities. He is not a race leader. He is a man for our times. History will remember him as a man who stood up and cast a hopeful vision for black America at a time when everything seemed hopeless."

—Dr. Carol M. Swain, author, public speaker, podcast host, and
former professor at Vanderbilt and Princeton Universities

Lessons From
—— the ——
Least of These

LESSONS FROM
—— THE ——
LEAST OF THESE

THE WOODSON
PRINCIPLES

ROBERT L.
WOODSON, SR.

BOMBARDIER
BOOKS

BOMBARDIER BOOKS
An Imprint of Post Hill Press
ISBN: 978-1-64293-647-6
ISBN (eBook): 978-1-64293-648-3

Lessons From the Least of These:
The Woodson Principles
© 2020 by Robert L. Woodson, Sr.
All Rights Reserved

Post Hill Press
New York • Nashville
posthillpress.com

Published in the United States of America

This book is dedicated to the grassroots Josephs who have passed on over the last two decades: Pastor Freddie Garcia—leader and founder of Outcry in the Barrio, Leon Watkins, Kimi Gray, Bertha Gilkey, Mildred Hailey, David Fattah, and my beloved son, Rob Woodson, Jr.—gone, but never forgotten.

Each, in his or her own way, helped me discover and gain invaluable insight into the principles presented in the pages of this book. If anything, I am merely an investigative journalist reporting on their brilliant innovations. It was their personal witness to these principles as much as their testimonies that opened my eyes and enlightened my understanding. Just listing their names together warms my heart, almost as if I could greet and embrace them once again.

CONTENTS

FOREWORD

**By William A. Schambra,
Senior Fellow, Hudson Institute**

My association with Robert Woodson, one of very few remaining prominent black conservatives in America, changed my life. In the most desolate, bleak, atomized and alienated neighborhoods, he finds traces of community and helps to nourish them.

As he argues, low-income people in the worst of circumstances—long after government and the free market have failed them—are able to come up with their own solutions to their own problems.

Whether it's a storefront church, or a boxing club, or a twelve-step group, they gather in community to meet their needs according to their values.

They are living evidence that the quest for community will, indeed, not be denied.

I was with Bob, Pastor Freddie Garcia, and Juan Rivera at their substance abuse program, Outcry in the Barrio, in San Antonio, Texas. I went up to Juan and described to him, with some puzzlement and perplexity, the deep refreshment and revitalization I always took away from these gatherings. I told him that I sensed that it was somehow related to the struggles that I faced in my own life—struggles different from his only because they occurred on the streets of more fashionable neighborhoods.

Pastor Rivera, the great minister to addicts, prisoners and prostitutes, put his hand on my shoulder and said gently, "Hey, you're one of us."

Me? Addict? Prisoner? Prostitute? *You bet.*

I may never have been addicted to heroin or crack, but had I not, in fact, been enslaved to the other legal, so-called acceptable chemical addictions? Had I not been hopelessly addicted at various points in my life to work, to scholarly credentials, to physical appearances, to professional success, political power, social status?

I may have never been a prisoner behind physical bars, but had I not been imprisoned within my own inflated ego, my exaggerated notions of who I am, what I can do, my false presuppositions and prejudices about what others can do and who they are?

I may never have prostituted my body for money, but, far worse, how many times have I prostituted my spirit, my very soul, to achieve petty recognition, to win applause from the crowd, to impress a boss, to win professional advancement?

Yes, I have been an addict, a prisoner, a prostitute.

What Pastor Rivera was offering me that day was infinitely more valuable than anything I could ever offer him. He was inviting me into his family, the community of the broken, the addicted, the enslaved; the community of those who had acknowledged and repented for their sin; the community of those who had found forgiveness and redemption and have summoned into their midst the healing presence of Christ.

This invitation to join the healing community of broken and redeemed children of God—that is what I sense whenever I am around the grassroots folks that Bob Woodson brings together.

That is what, every time, without fail, sends me away spiritually refreshed, renewed and healed.

You would think that this invitation would be irresistible to everybody…that mainstream America would come flocking. *That is hardly the case, because the critical first step involves admitting that we are indeed broken, that something is seriously wrong, and that we are helpless and our lives are out of control.*

Now just think of how much of our time and energy, as individuals and as a society, is devoted to preserving the illusion that nothing's wrong, that everything is okay, that everything's under control. If only we have the right IQ, go to the right school, get the right grades, have the right job, nothing can touch us. We'll be in control and in charge of our own lives and destinies.

And when things go very wrong, and we're finally confronted with irrefutable evidence of brokenness, not to worry—we can always rush over to the altar of science. Just as we seem to believe there's no physical malady that can't be cured through medicine, so we seem to think there's no emotional or spiritual malady that can't be cured through psychology or sociology or some other social science. All we need is a government willing to buy us enough therapeutic experts.

Given our huge investment in the illusion of our own omnipotence, no wonder the message of grassroots leaders as the answer to society's darkest issues isn't particularly popular.

Grassroots leaders don't talk about dysfunction and pathologies and being "at-risk," all of which suggest material deficiencies that can somehow be redressed by government or science.

They talk, instead, about brokenness and redemption—all of which suggest that we're helpless on our own and that we must look beyond our mere human powers if we are to be healed.

I have spoken with businessmen and professionals who have been wonderfully successful at what they do. They make a lot of money. Suddenly, they arrive at middle age and realize that something fundamental is missing. These people come to feel that they're called to offer their wealth and social skills in the service of some higher purpose. Yet they know that getting involved with big top-down, bureaucratic charities will not suffice, because those kinds of organizations don't fight poverty any more effectively than they create wealth.

They're searching for something else.

I have spoken with young people who tell me they want to devote themselves to a cause, to an undertaking that will give their lives a real sense of meaning and purpose. All the great secular ideologies, which in previous decades might have spoken to that youthful yearning, have dried up and collapsed. They proved to be gods that failed.

They're searching for something else.

And I have spoken with quietly faithful Christians who, at some point or another in their lives, find themselves living the experience of Jacob. Like Jacob, they found themselves alone in their tent one night, in the dark night of the soul, wrestling with God. For some, it was an addiction or alcohol dependency. For others, it was the tragic death of a loved one, or losing a job, or a divorce. With the grace of God, they came away from those struggles, blessed, like Jacob. But, like Jacob who was smitten on the thigh, they will forever walk with a limp. No longer are they into appearances, or into facades of perfection, or in denial.

They're searching for something else.

Let those searching for servanthood now bring their wealth, their professional skills, their dedication, their energy, their humble and open hearts, and offer them as gifts to our

faithful grassroots leaders as we seek their assistance and counsel in the restoration of our nation's healing communities.

Some Americans would like to experience that sort of community, but they don't think it's possible anymore, given the advanced deterioration of our civic institutions. They're full of despair and resignation. They look at the dry and scattered bones of our families and our neighborhoods, and they say, "Surely, no one can breathe life back into these lifeless bones."

Tell that to Freddie Garcia. Tell that to Juan Rivera. Tell that to Bob Woodson.

Every day of their lives, these extraordinary and remarkable men and women take the broken bodies of addicts, prisoners, and prostitutes and breathe the life of Christ back into them. They take abandoned and boarded-up homes and build joyful temples of worship. They take run-down corner taverns and build senior citizen facilities and day care centers. They take abandoned stores and build diners. They take cast-off factories and build incubators for new businesses. They take the empty lots and the glass-strewn streets of the inner city and rebuild healthy, vibrant, close-knit neighborhoods.

Grassroots leaders have been able to accomplish so much in their neighborhoods with virtually nothing by way of assistance and support from the larger society. None of their renewing work depends on passing laws, or winning elections, or raising or lowering taxes, or persuading some stubborn government bureaucrat to cooperate.

This is civil society, using its own spiritual and moral resources to heal itself. All that is required is for us, one by one, to start heeding God's call to his children to confess their brokenness and come together in community.

If we form this communion, not only will our low-income communities revive, and not only will our civic institutions rise from the ashes, but more and more so-called mainstream Americans will experience the same healing and transformation that I find here.

Indeed, I am still drawing sustenance, and insight, and healing, from the moment that Pastor Juan Rivera put his hand on my shoulder and said simply, *"Hey, you're one of us."*

America must recognize and expand on indigenous self-help neighborhood efforts. The originators of these self-help programs have unique firsthand knowledge of the problems and resources within their communities. They have established track records for solving social problems by motivating their communities to develop innovative solutions to unemployment, substandard education, teen pregnancy, gang violence, day care and other sources of community travail.

Robert (Bob) L. Woodson, Sr.,
President and Founder of
The Woodson Center

A Note from Bob

As a Black man who grew up primarily in a low-income neighborhood, I am well aware of the legacy of slavery, Jim Crow laws, and legalized racial discrimination. My mother was one of the many Black parents from that era who told me that I would have to work twice as hard in order to prove myself. I took her advice and did just that, putting myself through school, serving in the military and leading various urban renewal organizations across my career.

Though I have witnessed and experienced incidents of racism throughout my 80-plus years, not once did I consider myself a victim. Never have I thought that my destiny was dependent upon others acknowledging their privilege or advantage through circumstances. In fact, I know from experience the only path for bettering one's self and one's life is through taking responsibility for one's own uplift.

This message is becoming lost in today's society, where tribalism is taking root along political, ideological, and racial lines and with each camp entrenched in bitterness and anger. Today's youth are being told that they are either victims of oppression or are oppressors themselves, purely based on their skin color. And it is happening in a time where people of all races in our country enjoy unprecedented freedom and opportunity.

But not all are faring well. Many are suffering in neighborhoods across our country—in cities and towns of all sizes. The $22 trillion that our government has spent on social welfare programs over the last 50 years has not moved the needle on ending poverty. The disintegration of the family, lack of economic opportunity, a substandard education system, gangs, violence, drugs and an overarching lack of hope define life for many in these blighted places.

It is clear we need a different approach…and I have found it where you would least expect.

Grassroots leaders who live in the most toxic, broken areas of our nation are solving the problems associated with poverty in ways that no faceless government program can. In many cases, they have perpetrated themselves the kinds of problems they are now solving. Nearly 80 percent have the title "ex" in their biography.

But the reason these grassroots leaders are effective is because **they are witnesses of transformation in their neighborhoods.** They also recognize that solutions are usually found among those closest to those suffering the problem. They may not have university degrees, but they hold doctorates in overcoming life's obstacles. And the foundation of their beliefs and actions revolves around the idea of personal redemption (and agency). **They reach out to those in need with the attitude and belief that people are capable of being agents of their own uplift.**

For nearly 40 years I have been identifying and amplifying the work these grassroots leaders do, walking alongside them, helping them be more effective in their ministering to people in their communities. In this book I distill the many lessons I have learned from working with these leaders into ten principles that you can apply not only to how you approach your own efforts to helping the poor but to your own life as well.

Now, let's get on with the work that needs to be done.

INTRODUCTION

My father was a gogetter.

He was a World War I veteran and the first Black to drive a dairy truck in Philadelphia. Unions were controlled by whites, and my father was the first to break in. He died when I was about nine years old, and I still remember his strength.

I was the youngest of five children, and we lived in a South Philadelphia low-income, blue-collar neighborhood, but it was a strong community. It was segregated, of course, but it was also incredibly close-knit. Every child could read, because we were made to read out loud every day as a practice of the Black-run public schools.

Back then, all of the stores within one block of our house were owned by Blacks, including the Jackson family. They owned and operated a laundromat on the corner. I remember that they had a Model T Ford, and they were the envy of the whole neighborhood. The Branch family owned and operated a candy store on another corner, and the Whitakers owned a busy dry cleaners. Their son Eddie was the lead newspaper distributor for our area, and he supervised all of the boys who were part of his sales force...

including me. Sadly, he was drafted into the Army and within six months we received word he was killed at a beach landing.

Saturday mornings were my very favorite. Men driving horse-drawn wagons filled with fruit, vegetables, and fish flooded the block with their wares. Women gathered to bargain for the best prices as they enjoyed passing around the latest gossip. It was like a huge neighborhood festival…and I'll never forget that joy and camaraderie.

Back when Blacks in America were in the grip of Jim Crow laws, had no political representation, and suffered gross income disparities compared to whites, we managed to maintain stable families, build hotels, create insurance companies, and own and operate our own businesses. The elderly never had to fear any threat of harm from their grandchildren as many do today.

Civil Rights and the Rise of Welfare

The 1960s brought about the momentous achievement of the Civil Rights Act which guaranteed equality for all under the law. It was a long road, but finally the stain of slavery and Jim Crow laws could begin (truly) to fade away. Though all knew it would take time for those wounds to heal, it was a resounding victory for Blacks and the country as a whole.

The Reverend Martin Luther King—whom I had the pleasure of meeting a few months before his death—led the challenges and debates within the movement regarding a course of action to address injustice. Never once was his goal to vilify white America and promote a narrative that condemns its founding principles and its birth defect of slavery as a chronic curse that has poisoned its soul forever. Like many leaders before him, he

fought to compel this country to live up to its promise of freedom and justice for all.

The 1960s also brought about social programs designed
to help the poor, especially Blacks in the inner city. The Great
Society promised to eradicate poverty by meeting all of our
(peoples') basic needs. But instead of delivering on its promise,
it did just the opposite. No one could have predicted the devas-
tation that would (be visited) come about, especially on (upon)
low-income Blacks from what was to be the helping hand of
government. It wreaked havoc on the very communities it was
designed to help.

Fred Siegel, of the Manhattan Institute, explained in his
book, *The Future Once Happened Here*, that radical liberal social
activists in the 1960s concluded that one of the ways to reveal the
moral shortcomings of capitalism was to flood the system with
welfare recipients. In detaching work from income, and thereby
diminishing men and the role they played as fathers, welfare
dependency, drug addiction, and school dropouts would increase,
and the institution of marriage would fail, ultimately "opening
[the nation up] to radical change."

Three great forces emerged that severely injured the poor
with a helping hand. The woman's liberation movement, the
Black power movement, and the civil rights movement all gave
the War on Poverty their silent consent. Welfare became (the)
a substitute for the nuclear family, denouncing the traditional
family structure as racist. The civil rights movement in particular
descended into a "race grievance industry" where it remains today.

The grand plan of the liberal social activists has largely
worked. Fifty years after the introduction of the Great Society, the
poverty rate is the same as it was in the 1960s. And worse, today's
inner cities are ravaged by drugs, violence, crime, and fatherless-

ness, and lacking in educational and economic opportunities that offer the pathway out of poverty. The decimation of the family—in particular the Black family—cannot be understated.

Those in charge of the poverty industrial complex administering the social programs of the Great Society largely base its success on the number of people served rather than the number of lives transformed. Worst of all, the focus of the poverty industry is on problems that are fundable rather than problems that are solvable. For example, 70 percent of the $22 trillion our government has spent on poverty has been distributed to social service institutions that "serve" the poor.

In other words, the poor have become a commodity, supported by a social program predicated on governmental custodianship. Food stamps determine what the poor are permitted to eat; public housing, where they will live; public schools, where their children will be educated; legal services, who their lawyers will be; and Medicare, who their doctors will be. People in these programs have no control over their lives; rather their fates are determined by those "in charge."

Once seen as a source of temporary help, welfare is now a "right" for the Black community. Even the idea of slavery reparations is resurfacing to compensate people who have never been directly affected by slavery from those who never perpetrated it.

Today, the majority of our society has been conditioned to believe that the cause of—and solutions for—poverty and other societal issues are beyond their control and lie outside of our communities. With a boost from liberal political interests, Black America and other minority groups protest to vent their frustration with their helplessness and demand a response from the presumed agents of control on the outside.

Victims or Aliens or Neither?

Former Secretary of the U.S. Department of Education Bill Bennett once aptly stated, *"The left sees the poor only as victims, while the right sees them as aliens."*

In an unexpected twist, both the left and the right see the poor as hopelessly lost in a sea of pathology with few personal redeeming qualities. They assume that the only hope of rescue will come from professionals and the intellectual elite, and they cannot or will not recognize the capacities that exist within America's low-income communities. The poor are sentenced to live within an isolated sub-economy, an experiment in socialism within America. They are treated as impotent, uneducated children, yet expected to function as responsible adults.

Patronizing voices resound from whites who seek to save Blacks from themselves and Black "spokespersons" who embrace an agenda of racial grievance and an identity of victimization. Both groups ruthlessly deceive those who listen, declaring that the disintegration of the Black family and community is the legacy of slavery and Jim Crow.

There are two ways to disempower a group of people. One way is to prevent them from competing for resources as was the case under Jim Crow laws. **The other way, which is much more insidious, is to convince a person that they do not have to compete and should expect to be dealt a winning hand based upon past mistreatment.** They are robbed of the will to achieve and to excel.

Many of today's Black spokespeople—who I call "race racketeers"—profit handsomely in terms of money and power by keeping race as a divisive, front-and-center issue. They peddle their messages of oppression and victimhood, asserting that America cannot be redeemed and instead must be made to bear bottomless guilt for the transgressions she inflicted via slavery. Along with their guilty white liberal enablers, and the media who promote both, they pose as the vanguard of today's civil rights movement. Race racketeers cannot resist the opportunity to seize the podium or highly-visible positions in marches and protests before returning to their safe, upscale neighborhoods.

On the other hand, people of good will, armed with noble intentions, can do great harm to people in need by their acts of crippling generosity and condescending assistance. Though they mean well, they are blinded by their good intentions and fail to recognize the problems they create when they, as outsiders, parachute in with solutions and then leave, thinking they've done some good. Dietrich Bonhoeffer, the martyred German theologian in his book *Letters and Papers from Prison*, once observed that one of the most difficult human tendencies to successfully confront is not malice, because malice can be confronted with violence. It is nearly impossible to confront folly.

When well-meaning outsiders come in to a struggling community, they often fail to recognize that people must be agents of their own uplift. It is tempting to become a rescuer, but the truth is that these neighborhoods do not need saviors from the outside but mentors from within who invest and stay. **Often the most effective leaders in struggling communities are those who have suffered and overcome the same problems afflicting those they serve.**

The Power of Indigenous Healers

Hope for people struggling in disadvantaged, struggling neighborhoods cannot come from the outside. It must rise up from within.

Low-income grassroots leaders, identified and supported by the Woodson Center, are these agents of effective change. They have overcome trials of their own and turned to lives of service. They have developed highly localized and effective programs as part of their church or community center—or sometimes even out of their homes—to do what is necessary to help their neighbors.

These men and women are transforming drug-infested, crime-ridden neighborhoods into peaceful residential communities. Others have been successful in helping people live a drug-free life, restoring families, and rebuilding their communities. Often, **they themselves once struggled with the very vices they now are helping others overcome.** They once were menaces to society but now are ministers and witnesses.

These men and women are quietly making a difference, working day after day to address their neighborhood's needs and empowering those who seem destined to a dismal future to reclaim their lives and rise up.

In direct contrast to the "race-grievance" and welfare industries, these people and groups have dedicated themselves to bringing solutions—never seeking the limelight or taking advantage of volatile conditions to engender funding opportunities. They are tightly focused on the people who rely on them for guidance and assistance.

In a sense, the qualities that make them effective also make them invisible to those on the outside. They have been engaged in life-salvaging outreach on an ongoing basis and do not cease their efforts even in an atmosphere of crisis.

While some see these life-changing organizations and individuals as isolated exceptions, we at the Woodson Center know—and can empirically prove—that this is not the case.

Over the past 37 years, we have mobilized thousands of grassroots leaders in thirty-nine states…grassroots leaders that are transforming life after life, community after community with long-term, generational solutions. Together, we *identify* and *deliver* those lost in our own communities who genuinely seek to be lifted up. We *educate* and *empower* volunteer community leaders as they help their neighbors *realize* and *experience* freedom from a generational cycle of poverty, apathy, psychological captivity, and the taking of young life. We believe the solution to *healing* our communities comes from *helping* individuals *discover* a meaningful purpose in life and *find* common ground with one another.

Throughout the country, thousands of other neighborhood organizations are winning the same victories through similar strategies. They are applying shared values and successfully reaching and transforming people that others deemed incapable of change.

The Woodson Principles

From firsthand experience with substantial, sustainable solutions to society's most devastating and seemingly intractable problems, the Woodson Center has distilled fundamental **Woodson Principles of Neighborhood Enterprise** that have served as key to the triumph over the isolation and hopelessness that lead to predatory and self-destructive behavior. These are the secrets of the grassroots leaders that are transforming lives in the most toxic neighborhoods.

Every life in every community has within it the capacity to improve itself. This is the central truth I have learned through my life's work; these pages provide the details and roadmap for changing lives.

Every one of the Woodson Principles is applicable from the highest-level of federal government to mid-level communities to personal commitments. These principles cut across race, gender, political, and socioeconomic class and form the foundation for overcoming poverty and overall division in our nation.

The Woodson Center has derived all of its knowledge and experiences through a lifelong journey of walking alongside some of the most creative healing agents in the world. These people inspire others by the humble genius of their remarkable recovery from misery and decimation. They seldom despair, never blame others, nor offer excuses for failures. In the darkest times, they cheer others on offering forgiveness even to those that have betrayed them.

In all the years that we have held conferences, get-away retreats and policy seminars, racial conflict never emerged as an issue at any of our gatherings. Whites from trailer parks, inner-city Black and Brown people, Native Americans and Whites from Appalachia all are in attendance, united in love for one another. **What they share in common is their joy in celebrating how God delivered them from their brokenness.**

The Woodson Principles capture how these grassroots leaders are witnessing to others in their neighborhoods, serving as antibodies to the societal ills that are decimating lives. They are helping others see the people they can become. They are providing an alternative message. They are living testaments to what works in relieving poverty.

How to Heal Neighborhoods and Our Country

At a time of growing tribalism, social fracturing at the altar of identity politics, and the denigration of traditional American values, America is in need of a revival. A moral brush fire needs to burn again and sweep across this nation and generate a return to the virtues of the best of our past, leaving aside the birth defects of our history. The enemies of America's future derive their moral authority by claiming to be the champions of the poor and marginalized minorities. **The real champions are the quiet heroes working within our inner cities, transforming lives one by one through the redemption of Christ and fellowship with one another.** The Woodson Center has been gathering these heroes for the past 40 years and can serve as the catalyst for an American revival.

The Woodson Principles of Neighborhood Enterprise

Competence

Look first among people suffering the problem for a solution. Then rely on the "uncertified" practical knowledge of those living in the same geographic and cultural zip code as the people experiencing the problem, instead of ivory tower ideas from distant scholarly experts. Certification is not always synonymous with qualification.

Integrity

Relationships are the necessary condition for transforming others, and trust is the common currency. Before you can help others, you need to uncover and acknowledge your personal motives and level of commitment. Then, seek out leaders that are moral practitioners of virtue, honesty, and integrity and who are trustworthy and honest. One test of their authenticity is if they willingly point to those who have been helped by them or their organization.

1

Transparency

Leaders willingly open up and share their triumphs over the challenges they have faced in their lives, describing how they overcame brokenness and suffering. This is how they build trust. They refuse to hide behind their pain or their pride, instead offering up stories of their struggles with humility in the interest of establishing trust. We are all sinners in need of a Savior.

Resilience

In searching for healing agents within toxic communities, study those who are "in" troubled circumstances but not "of" those circumstances—those who have managed to survive and thrive If 70 percent of parents have troubled kids, study the 30 percent who have successful, healthy children to discover the secret of their success.

Witness

A witness is more powerful than an advocate, because witnesses live by the values they convey to others. Look for those who have overcome hardship. They possess more credibility with the lost and struggling than the most pedigreed, accomplished experts. For example, those who are in recovery from an addiction are living proof that recovery is possible.

Innovation

In our market economy, just three percent of people are entrepreneurs, but they create 70 percent of all new jobs. In like manner, a small percentage of social entrepreneurs can generate large-scale changes and improvements in the social economy, and their innovative ideas are by far the most effective. Empower the leaders and leverage the skills that are already available in the neighborhood.

Inspiration

You can learn nothing from studying failure except how to create failure. Begin your inquiry by recognizing the capacity people possess. People are inspired to improve when they are presented with victories that are possible, not injuries to be avoided. Provide them with the tools for self-determination and help them strive to succeed above all reasonable expectations. Then, look for ways to celebrate even modest improvements.

Agency

No one should have to surrender his or her dignity as a condition for receiving help. Unconditional giving leads to pity rather than the desire to succeed. People should be agents of their own uplift. Never do more for them than they are willing to do for themselves. There must be reciprocity as the framework of any meaningful relationship. In other words, a person should be given the opportunity to give in return for what is received.

Access

Eliminate barriers to access and serve all who suffer. Support positive incremental change through flexible options, not directives. Always strive to be "on tap and not on top." Expectations in the absence of opportunity are restrictive. People must be given the tools to take advantage of the opportunities presented to them.

Grace

Love and respect others, even when it's inconvenient. Look at neighborhoods as filled with people who have potential, not dysfunctional victims. The foundation of grace is radical forgiveness; a refusal to be held back by what used to be a hindrance in your life, real or imagined. Be free of bitterness, regret, and uncertainty about the future.

The Woodson Principles were distilled from nearly forty years of hands-on experiences with grassroots leaders, people who are embedded in communities struggling with social, economic, and spiritual problems. As a team, we study, reflect, and extract the wisdom that comes from this extraordinary, effective source of knowledge.

Woodson Principles in Action

The Benning Terrace Public Housing complex in Washington, D.C. was a notorious killing field. Back in 1998, 53 murders had occurred in two years—within the five-square-block complex.

Police were fearful of venturing into the community. Streets were deserted. Playgrounds were empty.

All of this changed when the Woodson Center partnered with a local grassroots organization, the Alliance of Concerned Men, who requested assistance in implementing outreach that would focus on reaching and working through the leadership of rival factions.

The Woodson Center helped the Alliance to intervene in the community. The members of the Alliance had a firsthand understanding of the conditions the youths lived in, having faced the same challenges. Because they had a long-term commitment to these youth and were available 24/7, they earned their trust. The Terrace gang leaders agreed to come together and meet at our offices.

After an hours-long meeting, remarkably, they agreed to a peace pact.

How did we know the truce was real? That the neighborhood would see long-term change?

People cannot be bribed into changing by offering them programs, nor can they be threatened with retaliation for their actions. Our grassroots leaders took the time to gain the trust and confidence of the neighborhood. They lived what they taught every day, right there, in front of everyone.

Shooting in the neighborhood ceased immediately. There was not a single gang-related murder for 12 years. The truce made headlines around the country, and authorities—including the Metropolitan Police Department and the D.C. Housing Authority—did what they could to support the newly-established peace.

Gang leaders and members who had once destroyed and divided their community joined together as the "Concerned Brothers of Benning Terrace" and seized the opportunity for productive engagement, ranging from graffiti removal and landscaping to serving as peer mentors.

These neighborhood leaders serve as healing agents. Their on-site, constant, personal outreach to troubled and predatory youth has had the remarkable proven capacity to transform violent gang members, helping them to redirect their lives and begin to serve as ambassadors of peace in their schools and neighborhoods.

The Origin of Transformation

Recognizing the unique, transformative capacity that exists within the population suffering the problem should be a key element of our nation's strategy to effectively address the tragedy of school shootings and youth violence…as well as poverty, broken families, and other afflictions.

The Woodson Center has established itself as a Geiger counter that knows how and where to find these indigenous healing agents and how best to support and strengthen them. We provide training and assistance to thousands of community-based organizations across the country, representing a broad cross section of racial, ethnic, and socioeconomic groups.

Real, lasting change begins in the lives of individuals, radiating out into our neighborhoods, our communities, and eventually, our nation. That means the challenge we face is both internal and external, and the responsibility begins with individual choices…*with us.*

WOODSON PRINCIPLE #1

Competence

Look first among people suffering the problem for a solution. Then rely on the "uncertified" practical knowledge of those living in the same geographic and cultural zip code as the people experiencing the problem, instead of ivory tower ideas from distant scholarly experts. Certification is not always synonymous with qualification.

The true anti-poverty experts do not have PhDs after their names—and often have "ex-"before them.

I remember a call from Connor Sweeney, former Speaker of the House Paul Ryan's chief of staff, asking if I could arrange for Paul to meet with a group of grassroots leaders in Cleveland. I said yes.

At first, I thought the Republican party was trying to see some people of color…so I made sure many of the leaders were white. Then the Secret Service had to screen everyone who planned to attend, because at the time, Paul was the vice-presidential candidate.

His staff came back with, "About three-quarters of the people you invited have criminal records." I said, "Wow. I thought all of them did."

We sat around the table, and the Secret Service was very uptight because we had guys with motorcycle jackets on and tattoos, some inner-city ex-gang members…just a vast variety of ordinary Americans.

Paul listened attentively for an hour, as they talked about how their lives had changed as a consequence of being redeemed and transformed by grassroots leaders in their own neighborhoods.

Usually, in Washington, they only do things when there's a political advantage. So, I asked Paul, "What's the advantage?" He said, "Well, I was moved by what I witnessed, and I want to learn more. I want to deepen my understanding on what really causes people to become transformed and redeemed, but I don't want any press. I just want to quietly go and learn."

So without fanfare and without press, Paul and I spent two years visiting different neighborhoods, learning how poverty can be defeated by the real agents of transformation who are embedded in low-income communities.

This is a completely new way to approach poverty.

We know all we need to know about the massive social and economic forces bearing down on the poor and making their ascent so difficult. **But why don't we talk to those who have made that ascent, and find out what routes they took?**

Without degrees, academic certifications, sociological, or policy expertise, they have found a way to bring about real-life transformation in their own communities, with their own neighbors.

The Largest Obstacle to Effective Change

We often assume that educated people are more moral and wise than people who are not educated. But I remember a university president several years ago who was arrested for making pornographic calls to female students. Friends of mine kept saying, "How could he do that? He has a PhD from Harvard?" I thought to myself, "So does the Unabomber."

Many of my grassroots leaders are doing fine things to transform and redeem people, but they are shut out from receiving much of the funding they need. It's not a lack of capacity or ability. It's the rules of the game. For instance, to qualify for many grants, you have to have a bachelor's degree.

Truly, **college certification is the biggest barrier to grassroots participation.**

Expert Opinion

I believe that the greatest obstacle to the efforts of grassroots neighborhood leaders is a pervasive elitism that obstructs a recognition of their unique capacities.

> *Unfortunately, many business leaders and directors of philanthropic foundations cannot seem to escape a mind-set which views low-income individuals as supplicants and applicants rather than full and vital partners in mutually beneficial efforts to generate the economic and spiritual renewal of our nation's neighborhoods.*
> —William Schambra,
> Senior Fellow, Hudson Institute

We tend to think that if a person is inarticulate, they are unwise. Nothing could be further from the truth. Part of listening to their language is refusing to be blinded by intellectual imperialism, where our education has convinced us that only people who are as lettered as we are know how to create change.

Grassroots leaders may not have degrees and certifications on their walls, but they do have this—the powerful, uncontestable testimonies of people whose lives have been salvaged through their work.

Listen to untutored people. They are in the middle of the battle and have more insight and wisdom than most.

Need Proof? Where Competence Succeeds

In contrast to many secular substance abuse programs that try to establish reputations for success by accepting only clients who have a good chance of recovery, most grassroots programs have worked with the people that all other groups—the churches, clinics, and psychologists and psychiatrists—considered to be hopeless. Their doors are open to those who are deemed "too far gone," or "beyond the age of rehabilitation."

Getting Personal

I will never forget the experience I had when I attended a conference of one grassroots, faith-based substance abuse program in Texas.

One by one, more than fifty men and women approached the microphone and stated only two simple but powerful facts: the number of years they had been addicted to heroin or crack, and the number of years they had been freed from their addictions through participation in that program.

It took my breath away.

Many of these former addicts have gone on to become the directors of satellite centers of that program and have helped salvage hundreds of other lives.

Today's successful grassroots leaders have embraced them all—prostitutes, thugs, those whom society has labeled valueless—and they have changed their lives. They reach people who come from the absolute abyss.

Among those I have met who have prospered through a second chance at life are a drug-addicted thief whose own mother slept with her purse under her mattress, fearing that he would rob her, and a heroin addict who "shot up" his own son when he was just fourteen—a son who by the time he was eighteen was serving time with him at the same penitentiary. These lives were salvaged. These people observed the difference in a neighborhood leader, trusted him or her, fought to overcome their struggles, and began lives of service. Each one has been awakened to their responsibility to themselves and to others.

From the Ivory Tower to the Streets

Professional service providers who receive funds in proportion to the number of people who are homeless, the number of youths that are engaged in violent inter-gang warfare, or the number of individuals who are dominated by drug and alcohol addictions have little interest in seeing these problems disappear.

Nor do they take kindly to embarrassing competition from untutored, non-credentialed grassroots public servants who consistently produce far greater positive results with a fraction of their budgets. Powerful political lobbyists, the professional "custodians of the poor," have continually attempted to stifle the efforts of neighborhood-based organizations, and even to shut them down through regulations requiring that any providers of services must hold advanced degrees or professional certification.

Along the same lines, professional sociologists and psychotherapists dismiss many grassroots successes in transforming wasted lives as simply the effects of isolated examples of charismatic leaders and go no further to probe the possibility of expanding and exporting their success.

Without publicity, professional credentials, or official endorsement, and with little or no public financial assistance, residents of urban centers have devised programs for children of their own communities, often dramatically reversing the rates of delinquency and patterns of gang warfare saddling their communities.

These grassroots activists and innovators, who live at the scene of the crime, who cannot and will not walk away from the problem, and who suffer most from the inadequacies of institutionalized controls, have mobilized their own resources and have achieved a measure of success with their intractable youth that would be envied in professional programs.

> ### Expert Opinion
>
> *In terms of the policy world, the way that we've tackled poverty for the last 15 years has diagnosed it primarily as a material problem. In the United States, in our very developed country, it is really much more about the breakdown of relationships and the breakdown of community. Often, that has material manifestations. But at root, it's something more complex going on. It's relational challenges. For example, if we want to tackle child poverty, we have to tackle fatherlessness. We have to rebuild the culture of marriage. We have to do everything we can to get out of the way of the people who are doing good.*
>
> —Jennifer Marshall,
> The Heritage Foundation

Founders of urban community youth programs are sometimes parents, but more often they are people who themselves have successfully survived the frustrations and temptations of ghetto living and the threats of minority status. They know personally what activates the struggling, violent young people in their midst. It is clear to them that the chance that a hard-core delinquent will be rescued emotionally or spiritually is greater when those who seek his rescue can authentically relate to him and he to them.

Practical experience shows that neighborhood people are uniquely able to provide the supportive and subjectively meaningful guidance required—outside of formal education

and expectations—so that their own youth can help themselves to wholesome maturity.

Woodson Principle #1

Competence

Look first among people suffering the problem for a solution. Then rely on the "uncertified" practical knowledge of those living in the same geographic and cultural zip code as the people experiencing the problem, instead of ivory tower ideas from distant scholarly experts. Certification is not always synonymous with qualification.

WOODSON PRINCIPLE #2

Integrity

Relationships are the necessary condition for transforming others, and trust is the common currency. Before you can help others, you need to uncover and acknowledge your personal motives and level of commitment. Then, seek out leaders that are moral practitioners of virtue, honesty, and integrity and who are trustworthy and honest. One test of their authenticity is if they willingly point to those who have been helped by them or their organization.

When I finished eleventh grade, I dropped out of high school and entered the military. I was assigned to Sampson Air Force Base.

For the very first time, I realized that Black Americans were not a majority. I met people who were white, Black, and Hispanic. I met a guy who used to be in Hitler Youth, a Jewish guy from Kentucky, and a mountain man from the Appalachians. It was a complete cultural shock to be around all these various people.

Never "Are You My Color?" But "Are You my Kind?"

The first time I saw racism in the raw, I was in Mississippi. A Polish friend, John Horneck, and I were getting ready to go into town to get a beer. We got in a cab on base, and soon as we got outside the gate, the cab driver pulled over and said, "I can take one of you, but not both of you." John and I had to separate.

I ended up spending my time with the Black G.I.'s, and he spent his time with white G.I.'s. We remained friendly, but racism limited our social life.

I watched how disrespectfully uneducated Blacks were treated in the south, and I said, "I'm no better educated than they are." I decided that if I wanted respect, I needed to improve myself.

So, one Friday night, I gave the keys to my car to my fellas and said, "You guys go ahead into town. I'm just staying on the base this weekend." I remember it was in Cape Canaveral, on a beautiful Florida night. Everyone was gone, and I went over to the library.

On Monday morning I began what the Army called "Operation Bootstrap." I went in to be tested, and I did really well, passing my GED and taking college courses.

Soon I was selected to go to an elite airborne electronics school. I was only one of eight people selected out of eighty to go for this training. I went to Keesler Field, and for six months I attended a top-secret training school where they wouldn't even allow us to take our textbooks home. They offered three hours of theory and three hours of practice on missile tracking systems every day.

The military gave me confidence that I could learn.

A group of engineers welcomed me into the staff control laboratory after training every night, and they began to teach me about how to process and apply the knowledge I was gaining. When my racist sergeant found out that I was doing extra studying, he forbade me from doing it. Then, he started flying me on days when I had classes at night—and that was just the beginning of his harassment.

Finally, I went to the inspector general of my squadron, Colonel Estunes. He told the squadron to not fly me on days that he knew I had class, which made my sergeant even angrier.

A man named Joe was supposed to administer my punishments. But instead of forcing me to clean an area over and over again, we played together on the squadron basketball team. Every night, when he was going to supervise my punishment, he would call me out to his office, close the door, and say, "Would you just turn on the game, run the buffer on the floor, and let's just watch."

For every jerk, I always met a "Joe."

People of integrity deliberately confront evil with the name of "racism." Of course, there are evil Black people and evil white people, just as there are honest, kind people everywhere. That's why I don't ask, "Are you my color?" I ask, "*Are you my kind?*"

It is sometimes difficult to be candid when you are in a situation when the expectation is to speak sentiments of racial solidarity. Living with integrity means that we tell and pursue the truth even when it is inconvenient.

Heroes and Healers

David Gilmour and I were "archenemies" in many ways. Because of his stance on government dependence, I helped remove him from the San Francisco Housing Authority. But one day he read the "Benning Terrace" story in the paper about the Woodson Center, Woodson Principles, and the communities we serve.

David decided to get involved with the effective change he witnessed...he became our champion in all levels of government. From encouraging leaders at the grassroots level to pushing hard for welfare and housing changes, David teaches and lives out his commitment as an advocate for the Woodson Center.

Regardless of our differences—David is white, Jewish, and liberal, while I am Black, Christian, and conservative—we love the young men we serve as sons.

He is "my kind." We established a relationship built on trust despite our political differences and began a two-decade-long friendship based on mutual respect.

Start with Yourself

One of my favorite authors and teachers, Charles R. Swindoll, defined *integrity* as "who you are when nobody's looking."

In other words, integrity means you are the same through and through, in every situation. It requires strong, solid character, a deep-rooted faith, and a commitment to do what's right, no matter the circumstance.

But where does integrity come from?

First and foremost, **integrity only develops through an intentional, internal transformation.** Men and women of strong character refuse to let external circumstances control their destinies: regardless of the odds they face, they refuse to accept the label of victim. They become dedicated to helping others in similar circumstances achieve productive, fruitful lives.

> ### Expert Opinion
>
> "It all goes back to truth. Some truths are universal, or at least Shakespeare said so; the Bible says things are universal. There are certain characteristics that human beings have, that are universal; one of them is integrity. If a dude's word is good, you can go anywhere on that dude's word. It's like having a credit card. It's as if you have an American Express card. You go in a store and show it; you are supposed to get some goods, and that is what it's about."
>
> —David Fattah,
> Co-founder of The House of
> Umoja, a grassroots organization
> combating gang violence

Next, I have discovered that *God never uses big shots; He uses broken people.* That's why attitude is the next indicator of internal strength and integrity.

We are in charge of our attitude. It is more important than the past, than education, than circumstances, than failure, than success, than what people think, say, or do. It is more important than appearance, giftedness, or skill.

Dr. Swindoll also said, and I've seen it enough to believe it: "Life is 10% what happens to you, and 90% of how you react to it." Your attitude also reveals your character.

Our Nation Was Built on Integrity and Virtue

On February 12, 1779, Samuel Adams, said:

> *"A general dissolution of principles and manners will more surely overthrow the liberties of America than a whole force of a common enemy. While the people are virtuous, they cannot be subdued.*
>
> *But when they lose their virtue, they will be ready to surrender their liberties to the first external or internal invader. For if virtue and knowledge are diffused among the people, they will never be enslaved. This will be their great security.*
>
> *For neither the wisest Constitution nor the wisest laws will secure the liberties and happiness of a people whose manners are universally corrupt."*

I believe that America's greatness is not defined by our military or our economy. Democracy and capitalism are but empty vessels into which we pour our values as a nation. That means the crisis that we face today is a crisis of values. Those of us who believe in these virtues are now part of the counterculture. It's time to move aggressively from the counterculture back into the mainstream.

However, it is not sufficient to oppose efforts that have failed in the past. Of course, that is necessary, but it is not enough. Neither is "caring" enough.

The all-too-common practice of declaring oneself morally superior by virtue of having cared more or cared earlier is insufficient. It is almost morally irrelevant in these critical times to declare that one cares! What matters is whether or not one has ideas and is prepared to act on them to improve the circumstances of the poor. Are you?

Woodson Principle #2

Integrity

Relationships are the necessary condition for transforming others, and trust is the common currency. Before you can help others, you need to uncover and acknowledge your personal motives and level of commitment. Then, seek out leaders that are moral practitioners of virtue, honesty, and integrity and who are trustworthy and honest. One test of their authenticity is if they willingly point to those who have been helped by them or their organization.

WOODSON PRINCIPLE #3

Transparency

Leaders willingly open up and share their triumphs over the challenges they have faced in their lives, describing how they overcame brokenness and suffering. This is how they build trust. They refuse to hide behind their pain or their pride, instead offering up stories of their struggles with humility in the interest of establishing trust. We are all sinners in need of a Savior.

I know sorrow. So do you. We all do.

Friar Richard Rohr taught that each one of us will experience a "disaster," or a critical moment that forces us away from immature attachment to power, wealth, or intellectual superiority. Whether it be death, illness, addiction, failure, or other manifestation of brokenness that forces itself, much against our wills, into our lives, this critical moment opens the path to a more complex and mature phase of life. We learn to accept imperfection and brokenness in our own lives and those of others.

Far too often, I see philanthropy and policy come out of unknowing immaturity. We design programs based on our own presumed superior intellectual or political status, designed to bring order and stability to the messy lives of those on the margins of society. Solutions seem to be simple, rational, coherent, and clear, just like our own lives…or so we think.

But when we are truly transparent, when we proceed from a place where we acknowledge that our own lives are complex, messy, and unclear, then we become open to the proposition that others are not incapacitated by their imperfections any more than we are by our own.

Grassroots leaders are masters of understanding the complexities of human nature. **They are fully open to the brokenness of human life because they themselves have experienced it.** They know all too well how messy life can be, how narrow the margin is between wise and foolish decisions, and what life can be like after self-destructive choices. That's why they are open and accessible to others whose lives have taken bad directions, and that's what makes them more successful at changing lives than their remote, rational expert counterparts.

But that is also what makes them suspicious to the "experts," who are forever searching for neat, rational, orderly approaches to human problems. The wealthy and powerful typically listen to the so-called experts, because experts in no way challenge the understanding of life as completely malleable through the application of money or political power.

Grassroots leaders by their very existence raise uncomfortable questions about this notion of the power of money and political position. But opening up to the wisdom of grassroots leaders is essential not only to public policy, but for our own spiritual welfare as well. These young people who find peace and meaning under the circumstances they have experienced have much to teach all of us.

I believe that begins with sharing our own experiences, our pain, and our sorrow. **It begins with transparency.**

Getting Personal

The late Michael Novak, world renowned sociologist and a former colleague of mine, joined me at a three-day Woodson Center retreat attended by over one hundred low-income grassroots leaders from around the country.

When Michael was describing his experience to a friend, he made the following observation, "Bob's people are not sophisticated enough to be deceitful."

I nearly fell off my chair laughing. His comment was and is a constant reminder of the profound difference between the world of Washington-based think tanks and their celebrity poverty experts and the real truth of those who live in low-income communities.

For most of my professional life, I have walked between these two worlds. My personal identity is more like an ambassador from "The Hood" to these salons of influence. I have friends in both worlds. However, my deepest friendships are among my grass-roots leaders.

If I woke up and found myself in a totalitarian state, I would feel safer in confinement with them that being free among the jailers. The reason for the feeling of deep kinship has nothing to do with race, and everything to do with character and transparency.

Racism Obscures the Truth

The issue of race is used as a smokescreen on both sides, hiding the real issues we face by fueling the growing divide that threatens to descend us into tribalism.

Fascists on the right claim to represent disaffected white people. Anarchists on the left purport to speak for the marginalized, minorities, and the poor. They battle it out over and over with the only outcome being more racial strife...and a misplaced focus.

In truth, neither the extremists on the right nor left truly promote the interests of the whites or Blacks and browns whom they purport to represent. Both groups denigrate the rich heritage of the founding virtues and principles of our country.

Conveniently airbrushed from the portrait of Black America are the remarkable models of self-help—accomplishments of Black entrepreneurs and mutual aid societies even during eras of the most brutal racial repression and slavery. The legacy of personal responsibility and principle-based entrepreneurship has fallen by the wayside, hiding the truth that could provide today's youth with pride in their heritage and a model that could guide them to a healthy, bright future.

The selective history that is transmitted to our young people is, simply put, that Blacks came to this country on slave ships;

from there they went to the plantations and slavery, from the plantations to the ghetto, and, finally, to welfare. That's a simplified version of revisionist Black history.

Most Americans—Black and white—are unaware of the number of slaves who, by virtue of their genius, determination, and effort, rose to become millionaires and made important contributions to society.

In the first 50 years after the Emancipation Proclamation, Black Americans had accumulated personal wealth of $700 million. They owned more than 40,000 businesses, and nearly a million farms. The literacy rate had climbed from five percent to 70 percent. Black commercial enclaves in Durham, North Carolina, and the Greenwood Avenue section of Tulsa, Oklahoma, together were known as the Negro Wall Street.

A complete, objective Black history would transparently reveal the truth that, even in the face of the most bitter oppression and bondage, many courageous Blacks persevered and accomplished, undaunted by the obstacles they faced.

Black Americans must stop hiding behind this false, shadowed narrative that our present-day problems are related to past injustices and instead take more responsibility for their predicament.

Getting Personal

When I appeared on Black Entertainment Television with Jesse Jackson, I referred to the strides that Blacks had made despite historical racial oppression. When I stressed that these achievements were due to hard work, not affirmative action, or "generous white people," Jackson disagreed.

> So I challenged him: "Are you suggesting that the destiny and history of Black America has been determined by what white America has allowed us to do?"
> His reply? "Abso-DAMN-lutely!"

Young people today have been fed a twisted ideology that has convinced them that their lack of achievement is solely the result of racism, which has limited their potential, justifying their rage, violence, and self-destructive lives.

I am convinced that the bondage of hopelessness and dependency can be broken by giving honest, transparent recognition to the Black heritage that was marked by determination, self-sufficiency, and achievement. We must expose the truth that strong families, religion, patriotism, and self-reliance are deeply rooted in authentic Black history. Again, Black America cannot hide behind the challenges of the past.

The False Front of Wealth

"Money cushions the wealthy from life." "Wealth greases the wheels of life...makes problems go away...opens doors into an exclusive world of pleasure and ease." "Wealthy people are greedy, selfish, and don't care about anyone outside of their exalted circles."

Most of us who live without wealth believe these myths wholeheartedly. They separate us from one another out of envy, anger, or simple misunderstanding. And they can ruin our relationships.

It's time to pull back the curtain and tell the truth. The rich face just as many problems as the poor. They're just different problems.

Money carries a heavy responsibility that can become a trap. Materialism never ever brings joy…only unhappiness and pain. Many children grow up in "gilded ghettos" with empty souls and ruin everything their parents build. The suicide rate among the rich is only surpassed by veterans suffering from PTSD.

Throughout the nation, there are many individuals who are wealthy and white and powerful yet are faced with emptiness and disarray in their personal lives. Many have children who are experiencing the same moral confusion that poor kids are feeling.

If some of the remedies to isolation and loneliness are similar to solutions that occurred in the low-income, toxic neighborhoods, perhaps low-income people can offer solutions to people in the upper classes as well. Perhaps we need to look for some new sources for a solution. **Perhaps if we were more transparent with those in our lives and worried less about appearance and what others think we could bless one another with more empathy and mutual support.**

Expert Opinion

In the book, *The Great Reformer*, Pope Francis speaks to the weakness of abstract intellectual approaches in addressing poverty:

> *Many of our political debates are so abstract. You cannot smell the sweat of real life, even though the healing of the body and the soul begins on the inside.*

He criticizes abstract intellectual systems that speak in crude generalities that instrumentalize the poor, using them as a means to an end, ignoring the unique nature of each soul and situation. Pope Francis challenges us to learn through intimacy...not just to study poverty, but to live among the poor. Or, I may add, at least *talk* with them.

Elites from both the left and the right are the primary sources of information that informs government, private foundations, and individuals about how and where to invest in poverty-fighting measures.

For decades, both sides have published bestselling books on poverty. Most of them concentrate their attention on documenting the pathology of the poor. They do not seem to understand that you cannot gain anything from studying failure. Ultimately, their lack of transparency—of objective honesty—blinds them to possibilities of deriving solutions from the community of people suffering the problem.

This is a deeper point of common concern and reveals the most fundamental need for the services that grassroots leaders can provide. They are able to show concerned and troubled middle-income parents, the leaders of corporations, and even the residents of lavish homes that echo with emptiness the message that, within low-income communities, there are remedies for the crises they are facing.

I remember when I took at the time vice-presidential candidate Paul Ryan to a meeting I had arranged at Cleveland State University with a roomful of participants, many of whom had criminal records. As Secret Service members looked on the room with stern eyes, each person shared their journey from troubled lives to ones of responsibility. The atmosphere began to gel and by the end of our meeting, the participants, arms bedecked with tattoos, asked if they could place their hands on Paul Ryan and pray for him. Not only was Paul moved, but there were tears in the eyes of the Secret Service agents. **Transparency begets openness and strong relationships.**

Along the same lines, grassroots healers can fulfill the role of a parent, providing not only authority and structure, but also the love that is necessary for an individual to undergo healing, growth, and development. Like a parent, their love is unconditional and resilient. They never withdraw their support, in spite of backsliding and even in the face of betrayal.

There will be many others who, in spite of their seeming success, will have the transparency, humility, and personal strength to admit, "I have some of the same failings and shortcomings that low-income people do. I am having the same problem with my own son or daughter: I'm worried about drugs; I'm worried about some of their activities; and I'm worried that he or she may be suicidal. I'm worried and I'm looking for remedies. If I can find remedies among the grassroots leaders in low-income neighborhoods, I'm going to look there."

Greater transparency—and a willingness on the part of the elites who study the poor to confess their own brokenness in the presence of grassroots leaders—would lead to better answers.

My colleague and friend Dr. William Schambra, renowned scholar and policy analyst, demonstrated by his actions how to cross this divide. Many years ago, he was one of four presenters on a Woodson Center panel along with grassroots leaders. He transparently acknowledged his struggles with alcohol abuse. After the tear-filled audience gave him a rousing standing ovation, he was immediately inducted into the family of grassroots leaders who also overcame this and many other personal challenges.

Ultimately, transparency breaks down barriers that separate people by class, by race, by education and creates a bond that enables each to join in common community to address the evils of the world. We have demonstrated in our work that our local leaders are united in their capacity to overcome brokenness in their lives and to celebrate and share with one another the process of redemption. This is what will unite this country.

Woodson Principle #3

Transparency

Leaders willingly open up and share their triumphs over the challenges they have faced in their lives, describing how they overcame brokenness and suffering. This is how they build trust. They refuse to hide behind their pain or their pride, instead offering up stories of their struggles with humility in the interest of establishing trust. We are all sinners in need of a Savior.

WOODSON PRINCIPLE #4

Resilience

In searching for healing agents within toxic communities, study those who are "in" troubled circumstances but not "of" those circumstances—those who have managed to survive and thrive. Learn from what has worked there and what has not. If 70 percent of parents have troubled kids, study the 30 percent who have successful, healthy children to discover the secret of their success.

When you go into a doctor's office, a credible, intelligent physician will first of all attempt to do that which is least intrusive to your body.

But traditionally, in our neighborhoods, we tend to apply the moral equivalent of a transplant. When government recognizes a problem, they do a drive-by analysis and parachute in a federal program, instead of looking for a remedy close to the problem.

At the Woodson Center, we go into low-income, crime-infested neighborhoods and ask questions that the professional service industry and scholars never ask of poor people. We don't ask them how many children are dropping out of school or in jail or on drugs; we want to know how many people are raising children that have *not* succumbed to the lure of drug addiction, have *not* become predators.

Once we find them, we apply "miracle grow" in the form of training and technical assistance. Then we introduce them to sources of financial support. We are able to grow remedies that are indigenous to these low-income, high crime neighborhoods by reaching out to grassroots leaders that are *in* poverty but not *of* poverty.

Who Lives "In but Not Of"?

Over the past 35 years, **the Woodson Center has demonstrated that the answer to the despair of inner-city Blacks is to help them become agents of their own deliverance.** Even in the most crime-ridden, drug-infested neighborhoods, there are people who manage to thrive. They were either immune to the temptation to the pathology or overcame it; they were *resilient*.

Consider that the reason that AIDS is so devastating is because it destroys the body's ability to heal itself. Our grassroots leaders are antibodies. They are indigenous to the body, to the community. They are closest to the source of disease. Therefore, if you strengthen the body's immune system, the body will heal itself and be resistant to future disease.

How do we find these healing agents? How can they expand to become an immune system? How and where do they exercise influence over others in their community?

We must go into barber shops, beauty salons, and grocery stores to ask people who they turn to in times of trouble. Many will identify the same people. When you knock on their doors and ask why they are sought out, you will find that they have given freely of themselves to their neighborhoods.

They will direct you to others like themselves down the block, up the street, or across town. When you assemble resilient neighborhood healers like these and support their individual and collective needs, the seeds of a grassroots movement are planted, which can transform an entire community.

Common Sense Commonalities

What these local healing agents have in common is the moral authority they exercise because of the trust they have earned from disaffected youths. These silent heroes represent potential new leadership to bring about the restoration of communities.

So rather than accept solutions parachuted in by middle-class professional service providers, Black America must recognize and expand on indigenous self-help neighborhood efforts. The originators of these self-help programs have unique firsthand knowledge of the problems and resources within their communities. In many cases, they were once menaces to society but are now ministers and healers.

They have established track records for solving social problems by motivating their communities to develop effective solutions to unemployment, substandard education, teenage pregnancy, gang violence, and other sources of community travail.

Heroes and Healers

Among the "Josephs" of Milwaukee, Wisconsin, are Victor and Dawn Barnett, who direct Running Rebels, a nonprofit dedicated to providing positive opportunities and models for youths ages 8 to 19 in their own neighborhoods and communities. These young people daily face the lures of drug abuse, delinquency, street violence, and teen parenthood.

Since its founding in 1980, the program has grown to include activities in the arts, sports, music and entertainment as well as job training and education. Essential elements of its outreach include cooperation with other groups in the community and the enlistment of the program's alumni as mentors to youths who are coming in and rising up.

On the basis of its track record of success, the courts and probation staff enlisted the Running Rebels to implement a program of "targeted monitoring" for young serious chronic offenders as an alternative to being placed in a correctional facility. Rather than identifying its participants in terms of their past offenses, the initiative focuses on the capacities and potential of the youth through a program of close communication with an assigned mentor.

Together, the groups are working to link and coordinate activities that offer year-round programs, exposure to career pathways and employment opportunities, and safe places where Black youth, at a critical stage in their lives, can receive support from older and young-adult role models.

Victor and Dawn have elicited trust and engendered the redirection of many of the youth they have served, notably reducing rates of recidivism. An analysis of impact revealed that the program has generated more than $63 million in savings to Milwaukee County from 1998 to 2012! More important, the program has made a life-changing difference for each and every participant.

Though the impact of Running Rebels has been remarkable, there are individual cases in which a participant does not successfully redirect his or her life and slides back into old ways. But like most neighborhood leaders, the Barnetts remain committed to these men and women, no matter what.

This was the case with a young man who is currently serving a life sentence. When regret and remorse resulted in his being placed on a suicide watch, prison authorities arranged for him to call the Barnetts, because they knew that the couple had provided the one oasis of hope and vision in the young man's life.

In that call, the young man apologized for failing to make use of the opportunity and guidance they provided him. Then, in a heart-wrenching moment, he pleaded: "Never give up on me!"

While this young man is destined for life inside prison walls and others might consider him beyond hope, the Barnetts and their counterparts throughout the country do not. They strongly believe that there is always hope and that no one is beyond redemption. They believe wholeheartedly in his resilience; his ability to survive and face the future.

Even though some of these young people are in impossible situations, like serving life sentences, the Barnetts never give up on them. Resilience and perseverance go hand in hand.

They never give up...and neither should we.

The Closer the Problem, the Closer the Solution

People who are surviving and thriving closest to the problem have the best chance of designing effective, long-term solutions.

In Flint, Michigan, political leaders failed to maintain safe water infrastructure for poor and Black residents. As a result, children and families drank water contaminated with lead, poisoning a generation. Elected officials at the state and federal levels did nothing.

Instead, local activists, doctors, and families exposed the contamination and forced the authorities to take action. Volunteers spread awareness about the risks of drinking tap water. Bottled water drives gave the community strength to withstand the crisis. Flint is not out of danger, but it is on a better path today precisely because its residents took on the challenge themselves.

The situation in Flint is a critical reminder that **the power of change is in the people affected by the problem.** The process of community organizing will bring forth the leaders who can truly represent their communities and advocate change, whether or not those leaders hold political office.

That's why we should look first to our neighborhoods, towns, schools, churches, mosques and temples to identify the leaders who represent our needs and values. Empower them, and the politicians will follow suit.

Failure or Freedom

To date, the anti-poverty agenda has been built on what I call "failure studies." Typically, researchers go into low-income neighborhoods to tally the youths who have dropped out of school, births outside of marriage, and incidences of gang activity and crime.

Then traditional programs, with their elaborate bureaucratic structures, with all their millions of dollars being spent to deal with these problems, fail again and again to effect change.

One of my grassroots leaders shared with me that the social workers are famous for that. They come into the neighborhood selling some lie and wonder why nobody will listen to them. I have personally heard of social workers being gagged and tied and put on a bus—and they were fortunate—and shipped back downtown.

In contrast, the Woodson Center goes into those communities to talk to the parents of families that are intact, the youth who have not been involved in substance abuse or crime, and the kids who have graduated from high school, to learn how they accomplished what they did in spite of the odds they faced...we identify resilience.

Their solutions apply to their neighborhoods far more effectively than anything we could do on a bureaucratic or policy level.

That's why we go into corner stores, barbershops, and beauty salons and ask the people who they would turn to in times of crisis. Invariably, they point to some person within the community that they can trust and rely on.

These "healing agents" exhibit common characteristics. They share the same geographic and cultural zip codes with the people they serve; they have a firsthand understanding of the challenges they face; and, they are available on a 24/7 basis and are committed for the long haul.

The testimonies of those who have been empowered to reclaim their lives through the work of these grassroots mentors are awe-inspiring.

Men and women who had virtually lost their lives to drugs and alcohol have emerged as responsible employees, spouses, and parents. Fatherless youth who were raised on the streets and were drawn to the lures of gang violence and drug trafficking have become agents of peace and renewal in their communities. **They epitomize resilience.**

People released from prison—with the mark of a felon and no prospects for a job—have risen to become successful businesspeople and entrepreneurs who provide employment to others in the community.

These agents of change and renewal not only have the potential to make a substantive and sustainable impact on the most entrenched poverty in this country but should be incorporated into the nation's anti-poverty agenda.

When we always study failure, we will always approach needs with pessimism, sure that we will solely raise the bar a notch or two. Frankly, when we create programs and policies from there, we will fail again.

But when we study resilience and look to the successes—with an optimistic perspective—we can build and support solutions that bring about real, lasting change.

Expert Opinion

Notorious gang leader Robert (Fat Bob) Allen had become a successful grassroots leader and agent for change in his community. He declared that, "We don't want anybody to give us anything or do anything for us, but we want help to do things ourselves. We can. And we will."

Fat Rob Allen died many years ago, but he came to live with my family for a brief period of time. Rob shared with me that Sister

Fattah, one of our grassroots leaders, helped him appreciate the value of a human life—his own and therefore others. Much of his fame and popularity with women, for example, was tied to his position as a gang leader. Once he left that lifestyle, he had to adjust and find an alternative to the kind of respect that came from being feared.

We helped him to become an ambassador of peace, intervening in gang disputes and bringing about peace. The pride he received from being feared was replaced by being honored for being a peacemaker.

Pessimism Saps Potential

Parents and Black community organizations are typically not consulted by professionals; nor do professionals expect to collaborate with untrained grassroots people who attack the same problems.

Accordingly, Black grassroots leaders begin their programs for youths in a context especially inimical to their efforts.

The effects of public policy often create unintentional—or even intentional—roadblocks to the efforts of neighborhood healers. Regulations on zoning, licensing requirements, housing standards, requirements for professional supervision of such programs, and lack of recognition and helpful cooperation from other institutions and agencies all create sometimes insurmountable obstacles.

Financial aid brings with it standards of accountability for dollars spent and an inevitable degree of outside interference, often by officials who either do not understand neighborhood dynamics or are unsympathetic to the work being done. No matter how successful or helpful a program may have been, getting money together to keep it going is always uncertain.

Not only do our neighborhood healers suffer from the lack of recognized, accredited status, but they also find that formal regulations may be impossible to meet when they are trying to solve community issues from within.

Finally, the professionalization of social workers, rehabilitation counselors, and court personnel has been taken as a license by these authorities to decide many things about the lives of others without consulting them.

Many professional workers enjoy power without accountability to those who become clients of their services. Paradoxically, local activists, solving their own youth problems, take on responsibility and accountability without authority.

As a result, communication between authorities with power and nonaccredited, responsible grassroots leaders with no power is continuously fractured.

I hate to see the knowledge and information and solutions to the problems at one end of the continuum, while the resources are directed at the other end. That must change.

I have met hundreds of dedicated grassroots leaders who have successfully addressed the most debilitating forms of poverty—that which are caused by the "choices people make and the chances they take," including the destructive and self-destructive behaviors of crime, addiction, and youth violence.

Prerequisite to addressing poverty is a revitalization of values and vision that dedicated, faith-inspired neighborhood leaders can, uniquely, engender.

The truth is, Blacks in the inner city are even more in bondage than they were 200 years ago. More than 3,500 children in Los Angeles under the age of fifteen ate breakfast this morning from trash cans. Gangs are a way of life…the only way to survive.

People are *in* **poverty, but not** *of* **poverty.** Poverty does not make you a thief or a drug addict. That's just a myth. The idea that poverty somehow causes you to become a predator and is simply not true.

Many people who are born into poverty have the desire to rise above it…to work hard and chase a better life. But too often, the obstacles seem—and the key word is "seem"—insurmountable.

Healing from the Inside Out

The rebuilding of any community has to begin with the restoration of its civic infrastructure. That means instilling personal responsibility, thrift, and accountability. When investment in human capital occurs, only then can economic development prosper.

In Hartford, Connecticut, in the 1970s, another dedicated neighborhood healer, Carl Hardrick, touched the life of Steve Holter, the leader of the city's largest gang, which boasted a membership of more than 600.

Steve's turnaround comprised two stages: First, he was able to redirect his followers and changed the direction of his gang's activities from violence and crime to community service projects; second and eventually, Steve became the co-president of a thriving construction firm. His relationship with Carl continues today, more than 40 years after his first outreach.

What is unique about Carl, Steve, and these other grassroots leaders is that they make a lifetime commitment to the young people they serve. It is not for the length of funded program. The agreement is, "If you commit to saving lives, I will commit the rest of my life to you."

I also recall a story from Carl about his relationship with his brother, who was savagely beaten by another man. Upon visiting him in the hospital, Carl found his brother was paralyzed from the waist down as a result of his injuries. His brother asked Carl to get revenge. As Carl left the hospital in a rage, Steve was with him and said, "If what you have been teaching me does not mean anything, I will go home and get my gun. But, if it does then you will call the police." It stopped Carl in his tracks, and he reported the crime to the police.

Although Carl Hardrick did not have a program targeted to strengthening and promoting marriage, his role as a surrogate father shows that even the lives of young men of a different generation who have suffered dissolution of their marriage can be made whole.

Policymakers and philanthropists who are concerned about the crisis of the family and civil society in America should put their expertise and financial support in the service of those who are on the ground, engendering transformation and creating islands of excellence in their community infrastructure, against the greatest odds.

How to Begin a Neighborhood Revolution

First, constantly look for leaders in your community, people who are surviving and thriving right where they are, social entrepreneurs who are making a difference on their own.

I comb through local papers, watch social media, talk with friends and family. **Discover who is already doing what you want to do…never import from the outside what already exists on the inside.**

I ask God to bring these agents of uplift my way through other grassroots leaders. If you really watch for them, you'll be surprised at how many neighborhood healers are trying to make a difference in their own way.

Ask these people who have successfully transcended their circumstances, "What worked for you?" "How did you do it?" "What kept you going when so many others haven't made it?"

Then act.

Help them to document what they're doing, to raise a little money, to recruit other volunteers. Don't try to change them or make them do things your way. Above all, they need someone to validate and support the actions they are already taking so that they can multiply the change!

Woodson Principle #4

Resilience

In searching for healing agents within toxic communities, study those that are in troubled circumstances but not "of" those circumstances—those that have managed to survive and thrive. Learn from what has worked there and what has not. If 70 percent of parents have troubled kids, study the 30 percent who have successful, healthy children to discover the secret of their success.

WOODSON PRINCIPLE #5

Witness

A witness is more powerful than an advocate, because witnesses live by the values they convey to others. Look for those who have overcome hardship. They possess more credibility with the lost and struggling than the most pedigreed, accomplished experts. For example, those who are in recovery from an addiction are living proof that recovery is possible.

The strongest witnesses, and agents of real change, are those who have lived in and come through anger and suffering. These grassroots leaders are deeply committed to change in their own communities, and as they live out their character- and life-transformation, they positively impact others.

Woodson Center Violence-Free Zones are bringing these witnesses into direct contact with the young people who are and will be shaping their neighborhoods for good or for ill. We place "youth advisers" into schools, where they infiltrate the culture of the people they serve. Many of them already have "street cred," or reputations across the community. They can connect with children and youth in a uniquely effective, authentic way.

In Violence-Free Zones, youth advisers spend the first several weeks simply welcoming students at the front doors. Then they are present in the halls, cafeterias and detention rooms. They're known, respected, and trusted by the students.

On one particular occasion, a youth adviser stopped a young man in the hall and asked for his hall pass. The boy explained that he was the head gangster in school, so he didn't need one. The youth adviser smiled and said, "There's a new sheriff in town. I'm the head gangster now."

Then the student said that his brother would "take care of him," and crossed his arms in a threatening stance. With a smile, the youth adviser offered up his phone. The student immediately dropped his arms. He recognized the adviser from the streets and realized that he knew his brother…his threat didn't mean a thing.

From that moment, the youth adviser built up a relationship with the student. Today, both serve as advisers in the same school!

Today, when a student smuggles a gun past school security, a youth adviser is alerted and the student is quietly removed from the premises and arrested, all without the school going on lockdown. When the youth adviser is alerted to an after-school fight, police and youth advisers are on the scene as the crowd begins to gather. They stop incidents before they happen.

As trusted friends, youth advisers also have access to students' social networks. This access is a vital component of violence reduction in both urban and suburban schools.

In 2004, the Department of Education and the Secret Service published a report reviewing thirty-seven school shootings and school attacks from 1970 to 2000 to determine if there was a common element in the shooters' profiles. There wasn't. But the study did reveal one element that was found in nearly all of the shootings: The killers had told someone in their social network what they were going to do.

This information was unavailable to authorities, who are not tuned into the wavelength of the youths' communication system, known on the street as "the buzz." Violence-Free Zone youth advisers fill this information gap and intervene proactively to defuse violent or dangerous situations.

The success of the Violence-Free Zone initiative is evidence that a key solution to the crisis of youth violence can be found among those who are suffering the problem.

Change by the Numbers

The Violence-Free Zone initiative in Milwaukee Public Schools is credited with helping to produce a 25-year low in violent incidents and a 25 percent increase in graduation rates. And today, the model of the Violence-Free Zone initiative is embraced by public school systems throughout the country and has been implemented successfully in some of the most dangerous schools throughout Dallas, Atlanta, and Baltimore.

Witnesses Live and Serve at Home

Leaders and politicians argue for solving poverty through greater representation of Blacks in police and government agencies.

Since the civil rights movement, Black leadership has not improved the conditions of minority neighborhoods. Current policy causes a bait-and-switch game, in that the "experts" who develop these systems are solely using nationwide statistics on urban minority young people to justify funding. That money is then given to organizations which do not traditionally serve individual communities or constituencies.

There have been many instances where grants were given to traditional youth-serving organizations to address youth violence or to provide service. In one instance a survey was taken of how effective the outreach was to youth in trouble. None of the youth surveyed had any knowledge of the groups that were originally funded.

The nation's war on crime is like seeing a fire and then proceeding to build a firehouse instead of getting water to put out the fire. **We must get down to the home-by-home, street-by-street level and strengthen our community institutions.**

As the country searches for ways to reduce youth violence, some answers are located where we least expect to find them—among the group experiencing the problem.

In high-crime areas, such as the neighborhood I grew up in, there were a disproportionate share of offenders. But there were also strong mediating structures, like churches, community organizations, and families, that should be mobilized to curtail crime and poverty alike.

I believe that every neighborhood is different, so the answers to these critical problems abide within the communities suffering from them.

Solving Issues Door-to-Door and Street-to-Street

Grassroots organizations have blazed new trails across Black America. As neighborhoods band together to control their own destinies, previously unused talents and resources are now being tapped to foster a climate of economic and social advancement in what had been considered to be human wastelands.

Nationwide, nothing could so strikingly emphasize this point as the emergence of public housing resident management corporations. In Washington, Boston, New Orleans, St. Louis, Louisville, Jersey City, Minneapolis, Chicago, Denver, Tulsa, Los Angeles, Kansas City, Baltimore, Pittsburgh, Houston—wherever public housing authorities have allowed residents to manage public housing units—dramatic changes have taken place.

Scores of small businesses and hundreds of jobs have been created, crime and vandalism have decreased, teen pregnancy statistics have been reversed, and fathers and husbands have returned to abandoned families. At the same time, administrative costs have been drastically reduced, apartments repaired, and rent collections doubled.

Resident managers have succeeded in instances where the private sector and government initiatives have failed. The key to this success is their firsthand knowledge of the problems, needs, and preferences of residents.

Heroes and Healers

Antonette "Toni" McIlwain is yet another modern-day "Joseph" who has been a catalyst for a remarkable revitalization of her Detroit neighborhood of Ravendale.

The neighborhood was deteriorating, getting more and more dangerous. Absentee landlords let their properties slide into irrevocable disrepair, and many abandoned them completely. Drug addicts stripped vacant houses of everything from plumbing and wiring to doors and windows. Crack houses multiplied.

One former dealer identified thirty crack houses in the thirty-eight-block neighborhood, describing one as a drug addict's version of a fast food restaurant: "You could get anything you wanted in any amount. You could use it there or do a carry-out." Out of hopelessness and fear for their own safety, the neighbors decided to just look the other way.

Toni had firsthand experience of individual transformation, and she also believed that community transformation could happen with determination and hope. She walked door-to-door, urging residents to turn out for a community organizational meeting to be held in her living room. She called out to neighbors who looked down from windows with iron security bars, and she repeated her message through the locked front doors of more timid neighbors.

On the night of the first meeting, Toni sat alone in her living room. Three subsequent meetings failed to bring the neighbors. However, on the afternoon of the fifth meeting, a friend loaned Toni a bullhorn, and she bravely strode up and down the streets, calling out, "Put down that forkful of eggs! Put down that newspaper you're reading! Come to the meeting on Wade Street, and we can change this neighborhood."

Inspired by a new sense of hope and community, the neighbors brought out rakes and shovels and brooms and paint brushes. In small brigades, they hauled litter and debris from alleys and cut back plants and grasses. With newly painted curbs, litter-free streets, and landscaped lawns, Wade Street stood in striking contrast to the rest of the neighborhood.

The city recognized them and responded with public awards, but little by the way of awards in the form of grants or other incentives. The Woodson Center was able to introduce them to a private corporation that provided funds to help them along.

> Under Toni's leadership, neighborhood residents continued to organize with block captains and special committees. As a result of their efforts, crime in the area has been reduced by 42 percent, drug traffickers have been driven out, and a community park now stands where the notorious crack house once operated.
>
> The well-lit, landscaped neighborhood bears little resemblance to the devastated, disinvested area it was before Toni planted the seeds of commitment and hope among her neighbors.

Healers Live Next Door

Neighborhood healers are witnesses both to the problems they live with, and of the success of their solutions. They are living, breathing examples of healing and hope.

They are also available. In contrast to a therapist who comes once a week for a forty-five-minute session, or staff who are there only from nine to five and then return to their distant homes, grassroots leaders are on call virtually twenty-four hours a day. Their very homes are open to the people they serve, who are seen as friends, not as clients.

The healing they offer involves an immersion in an environment of care and mutual support with a community of individuals who are trying to accomplish the same changes in their lives.

A mentor comes at a predestined time and stays for a limited period of time. **Someone who is a witness is there all the time, in good times and bad.**

Down to the Local Level Every Time

The current foster care system destroys children caught up in its web. Over 70 percent of all people in our nation's prison system have spent some time in the foster care system. Large numbers of homeless youth have aged out of the system. When they reach age 18 they are no longer wards of the state and therefore the government stops making payments to foster parents for their upkeep. Many are put on the streets. Foster children are also a source of child sex trafficking. Our foster care system is filling the pipeline to prison far more quickly than our nation's failing schools.

Community- and faith-based organizations have recruited volunteers from within local neighborhoods to host struggling families during crises, and prevent children's entry into the foster-care system and facilitate timely adoptions. These are the best witnesses.

Harvest of Hope in New Jersey connected with the local church to address the shortage of Black foster care homes. Over fifty drug addicted mothers had abandoned their newborn infants in the hospitals as they registered under a fake name. They were called "Boarder babies." The Harvest of Hope connected the church with state social services to take in the babies and place them with members of different congregations. To date all these babies have been adopted. Thus, Harvest of Hope helped the church become a foster care program. Now, they have successfully placed more than 1,400 children in local, loving homes and facilitated 300 adoptions.

Because most such effective organizations exist within the neighborhoods they serve and work without fanfare, we need to take an inventory of similar programs that work within their individual communities.

Congress could play a role by passing outcome-focused legislation to address the foster care crisis. To this end, the Family First Prevention Service Act passed recently prioritizes keeping children in stable homes by providing help for families struggling with drug addiction or other self-destructive behaviors. It also provides states with incentives to reduce the institutionalization of children in group homes that are not only expensive but associated with lower academic achievement and higher risk of delinquent behavior.

I believe that we should ensure that this law and other similar initiatives realize their promise by establishing an alliance of private-sector groups to work with five state governments to reduce their foster care population by 50 percent. On the foundation of that pilot initiative, the program could spread throughout the country.

The Power of Living "New"

Unlike the popular programs espoused by policymakers and academia, the impact of inner transformation lasts a lifetime. Hyper-local, neighborhood-based, witness-oriented programs inspire transformation. They do not simply curb deviant behavior but offer something more—a fulfilling life that eclipses the power of temptation.

Heroes and Healers

In Washington D.C., Bishop Shirley Holloway includes marital and premarital counseling in the House of Help and City of Hope Ministries she launched to empower homeless men and women to reclaim their lives. More than 100 couples have come together and married through Holloway's ministry.

Angela entered the program as a mother of two and an addict who was on the street, struggling with deep depression. James

Woods had just been released early from a 20-year prison term for dealing drugs. He wasn't sure how to start over.

Then as the two rebuilt their lives, they became a couple and were married in 2000. Their union benefited from the pre-marriage counseling and financial guidance provided by the ministry.

Today, the Woodses have five children and four grandchildren and are proud homeowners. They serve as a couple within Bishop Holloway's ministry, working to uplift the lives of others. They are witnesses to the power of personal transformation and their turnaround has had a ripple effect in their community.

When transformed individuals reenter their old environments, many have the power to change those environments... bringing real hope and healing to their neighborhoods...and to our nation. **Leaders can play a critical role in their own protection, by living out their transformed lives in front of others. This demonstrates once again the power of a witness.**

Woodson Principle #5

Witness

When searching for witnesses, look for those who have overcome hardship. They possess more credibility with the lost and struggling than the most pedigreed, accomplished experts. For example, those who are in recovery from an addiction are living proof that recovery is possible.

WOODSON PRINCIPLE #6

Innovation

In our market economy, just three percent of people are entrepreneurs, but they create 70 percent of all new jobs. In like manner, a small percentage of social entrepreneurs can generate large-scale changes and improvements in the social economy, and their innovative ideas are by far the most effective. Empower the leaders and leverage the skills that are already available in the neighborhood.

I identified deeply with a study I read years ago from David Birch at the Massachusetts Institute of Technology. He discovered an interesting pattern; A students tend to come back to universities to teach, but C students come back to endow the university for future generations.

My experience says that very smart people have all the answers. But by the time they act, the opportunity is gone.

However, the "average" person simply acts on the knowledge he or she does have and risks failing. Then they come back a second time and a third…perseverance is far more important in an entrepreneur than anything else.

Understand this; commercial entrepreneurs only make up three percent of the population, but they generate 70 percent of the jobs.

I believe the same phenomena occurs in our social economy. **A small percentage of people create programs and approaches that transform and redeem people. What they generate and what they produce will change a whole community.**

That's why I am a huge advocate of taking the principles that operate in our market economy and applying them to our social economy—success is defined by what you produce that's of value to people.

In other words, no one cares whether Bill Gates has a degree or not, as long as he's producing something that people will buy. The same is true in our social economy. When grassroots leaders are making a positive impact through an innovative approach, they deserve investment. They are producing something that's of value. Often, they achieve these substantial and lasting trans-formations at only a fraction of the cost of less effective but "cre-dentialed" programs.

Practical Help for Practical Change

People who are healing agents are like social entrepreneurs, they need help that enables them to do more of what they do.

In other words, we should act like social venture capitalists, always looking for honest entrepreneurs who are already making progress in their own neighborhoods. Frankly, they tend to be poor administrators. **You will make the biggest difference by not just bringing in capital, but also training, guidance, and expertise.**

In my experience, growth needs to happen along a continuum, not too big and not too small at first. Help these entrepreneurs handle the amount of capital and apply it wisely, so that you don't outstrip demand and help too much.

You are helping your social entrepreneur "take their product to market"…watch the change happen.

Are You a Pharaoh or a Joseph?

Joseph was one of twelve sons of Israel. His mother died as she gave birth, and Joseph became his father's best-loved son. Joseph's brothers had always been envious of him, but when he related a dream in which they bowed in supplication to him, their anger ignited, and they conspired to kill him.

One day, when they were far from home tending sheep, the brothers seized Joseph and threw him into a pit. While they were arguing about how to dispose of him, a caravan of Ishmaelites passed by on their way to Egypt. The brothers agreed to sell Joseph as a slave to these traders rather than killing him.

To explain Joseph's disappearance, they took a cherished cloak that had been given to him by their father and soaked it in the blood of a sheep as evidence that Joseph had been attacked and killed by wild animals.

While Israel mourned his son, Joseph was sold in Egypt to the Pharaoh's personal assistant, Potiphar. Joseph embraced his fate and served faithfully and diligently in Potiphar's household. In return for his loyal service, Joseph was eventually appointed supervisor over all Potiphar's servants and became the chief administrator of his household.

In spite of his purity, Potiphar's wife began to lust for Joseph who was handsome and young. Joseph rejected her seductions, proclaiming, "My master trusts me with everything in the entire household. He has made me equal in authority and has held back nothing from me other than you, his wife. How could I do such a wicked thing as to violate his trust? It would be a great sin against God!"

In a desperate effort to get away, Joseph fled the house, leaving behind the cloak that his master's wife had torn from him. In retaliation for this rejection, Potiphar's wife claimed that Joseph had attempted to rape her and used the cloak as evidence against him. Joseph was apprehended and imprisoned.

Even in the depths of the dungeon, Joseph accepted his fate and served faithfully. He was, even in prison, raised to a position of leadership and placed in charge of the other prisoners.

Two of the Pharaoh's servants who were also imprisoned at that time on charges of theft learned of Joseph's ability to interpret dreams and beseeched him to explain their dreams, promising that, in return, they would help him after they were released. On the basis of their dreams, Joseph correctly predicted that one of the servants, a cup-bearer, would be released and promoted and that the other, a baker, would be hanged.

The servant who was released soon forgot his promise to help, and Joseph remained in prison. It was only years later, when the Pharaoh himself was troubled by ominous dreams which none of his counselors or astrologers could interpret, that the servant told him of the Hebrew boy and his ability to decipher dreams. Joseph was summoned to the Pharaoh's court.

When the Pharaoh described his dreams, Joseph replied that they were portents that seven years of bountiful harvest would be followed by seven years of famine. He advised that, during the prosperous years, one-fifth of all that was produced should be stored in preparation for the famine and that an administrator should be appointed to oversee this effort.

When the famine came, the Pharaoh's was the only land that was prepared. The Bible recounts that Egypt not only survived the famine but prospered for four hundred years until "there arose a Pharaoh who knew not Joseph."

Although Joseph was betrayed and treated unjustly, he always held firmly to the belief that God could work through any situation, and even in the worst circumstances he continued to serve without resentment. He never yielded to bitterness and his attitude determined his availability to God.

Heroes and Healers

Today, in communities throughout the nation, hundreds of "modern-day Josephs" and grassroots leaders are at work, restoring spiritual health in their neighborhoods, guiding others to lives of value and fulfillment.

The House of Umoja, founded by Sister Falaka Fattah, used the African extended family model to successfully reduce gang

violence and delinquency among troubled Black youth in Philadelphia.

Counseling, peer group discussions, and shared activities were
regular exercises that cemented relationships by cooling down
hostilities and anxieties. Sister Fattah also pioneered a group
house concept, with a central authority figure, that designated
areas of responsibility for each inhabitant.

The results were so dramatic that Philadelphia's criminal justice system tapped into the resources of the House of Umoja by
referring delinquents directly there rather than isolating them in
area reform schools and detention centers.

When policymakers recognize the effective functionality
neighborhood leaders can create, positive change is the result...
I've seen it over and over again. So why don't we make that our
move every time?

No matter how wider society responds, today's Josephs face
adversity and injustice without bitterness or resentment. They
embrace individuals that all the conventional service-provid-
ers—from government aid to charities—have given up on. **They
love the lowest of the low, embrace the worst cases, and meet
people right where they are...and their effectiveness blows all
other kinds of help out of the water!**

Meet the Pharaohs

The Pharaoh was not deterred by the fact that Joseph was not
of the same background, that he came from a "dysfunctional
Hebrew family," or that he was a prisoner. He trusted and followed Joseph's advice, and even appointed him to administer his
harvest, awarding him power of office second only to his own.

When the famine came, the Pharaoh's was the only land that was prepared. The Bible recounts that Egypt not only survived the famine but prospered for four hundred years until "there arose a Pharaoh who knew not Joseph."

Today's Pharaohs are the resource-holders, those who hold the keys to wealth and have the ability to deploy it when and where it can make a difference in our nation. They are deeply committed to the needs of others above and beyond their own. But the strength of their character lies not simply in a heart of compassion and a deep dedication to generosity, but in the commitment to act.

In addition to leaders of the business community who have a material, financial incentive to enter such a relationship, there are pharaohs who may not have wealth but have standing in the academic and political communities, who can be powerful policy advocates. They are like ambassadors. These pharaohs have the ability to perceive the internal, spiritual resources that grassroots healers possess.

Their wisdom applies beyond the borders of the troubled neighborhoods they serve. They can be the voice that educates middle- and upper-income white America about the important role that the Josephs can play, not only in their own neighborhoods but also in the personal lives of the occupants of the gilded ghettos of our society.

Change by the Numbers

Prior to involvement with the Woodson Center, the Lynde and Harry Bradley Foundation made very conventional local grants, largely benefiting established institutions of higher education, hospitals, and conventional social services organizations.

When they became aware of the Woodson Center and its innovative approaches to addressing poverty by empowering grassroots leaders, the Foundation began to employ the Woodson Principles to discover "Josephs" in their home city of Milwaukee, Wisconsin. More important, they became partners, identifying homegrown agents of transformation...agents who would indelibly impact their neighborhoods.

The Foundation's tradition of providing philanthropic support according to the Woodson Principles has continued more or less unaltered for more than twenty years, with the Woodson Center offering advice, support, and immersion in a community of like-minded people.

As a result of this longstanding partnership, the Bradley Foundation has made hundreds of grants to Milwaukee-based grassroots and faith-based groups offering community-based, self-help-oriented solutions that effectively address social issues others regard as intractable. The sum of these grants exceeds $100 million and the lives affected number in the thousands!

Together with the Woodson Center, these pharaohs are elevating the work of innovative, credible, creative leaders—Josephs—who are morally compelled to solve problems in their own communities.

Connecting the Pharaohs and the Josephs

I believe that relationships are the foundation of all change. Connecting the Pharaohs and the Josephs is the beginning of recalibrating our society, giving those within struggling communities the resources to change...and the support to do it in their own, innovative way.

But today's Josephs often go unrecognized, unappreciated, and underutilized. Our society dismisses the truth that neighborhoods and individuals in distress have the ability to help themselves.

That's where our pharaohs come in. They have open minds and hearts to learn. They are willing to see that low-income or troubled neighborhoods can raise up leaders from inside…leaders that can bring about lasting change. And they give.

They give with passion. They give with determination. They give with strong belief in today's Josephs and trust them to bring about positive, long-term, generational change. They are often entrepreneurs themselves and recognize innovation when they see it.

Woodson Principles in Action

Twenty years ago, when I met Pastor Freddie Garcia and his wife in San Antonio, Texas, he and his wife had just started a ministry called Outcry in the Barrio. They were recovered drug addicts, and they committed their lives to help others overcome their addictions.

Now, we are talking the lowest of the low, the worst cases that you can possibly imagine. And back then, all they had were little wooden barracks to house people.

I brought together ten of my pharaohs for a meeting in Dallas. One of those funders heard Freddie's vision and committed a million dollars to help Freddie build a real facility for the ministry. His lead gift inspired several other wealthy Christian businessmen in San Antonio to get involved, and over the next three years we built a brand-new $3.2 million facility in the lowest-income area of the city. To date this facility has changed thousands of lives.

I remember one specific story that really shows what God has accomplished there. Toni, one of my top grassroots leaders in Detroit, picked me up at the airport. On the way through her neighborhood, a young woman came over to talk to her at a traffic light. She was very thin and gaunt looking, clearly high on something. Then Toni introduced her; "Bob, I want you to meet my youngest daughter."

As we drove away, Toni was in tears. She said, "Bob, my daughter is sleeping in an abandoned car four blocks from my house. We have custody of her two daughters. I have helped hundreds of kids over the years, and I can't even help my own daughter."

I arranged to send Toni's daughter to Outcry on a one-way ticket. Two staff members met her at the airport and took her to the women's dormitory. Within six months, Toni had to send her daughter new clothes because she had gained so much weight. Six months later, she returned to Detroit, a transformed and redeemed soul. Today, she has regained custody of her daughters.

Now, after fifty years of service, Outcry in the Barrio has spread to sixty-five satellite centers in California, Texas, New Mexico, Peru, Puerto Rico, Mexico, Colombia, and Venezuela. To date, they have helped thousands of drug abusers and alcoholics overcome their addictions for good.

All of the pharaohs gave anonymously, not expecting anything in return. And every bit of what they gave has been returned a thousand-fold in changed lives.

At the crossroads of our nation's destiny stand two figures—Joseph and the Pharaoh. Both are men of strongest character and determination.

One possesses the commitment, understanding, innovation, and heart that can guide individuals to lives of spiritual health, fulfillment, and service; the other possesses the resources, power, and influence that are necessary to support, export, and expand that mission of revitalization and salvation.

If, today, pharaohs can emerge who have the humility and wisdom to embrace and support faithful innovators like our modern-day Josephs, like ancient Egypt our land will prosper for four hundred years—and beyond.

Which one are you?

Woodson Principle #6

Innovation

In our market economy, just three percent of people are entrepreneurs, but they create 70 percent of all new jobs. In like manner, a small percentage of social entrepreneurs can generate large-scale changes and improvements in the social economy, and their innovative ideas are by far the most effective. Empower the leaders and leverage the skills that are already available in the neighborhood.

WOODSON PRINCIPLE #7

Inspiration

You can learn nothing from studying failure except how to create failure. Begin your inquiry by recognizing the capacity people possess. People are inspired to improve when they are presented with victories that are possible, not injuries to be avoided. Provide them with the tools for self-determination and help them strive to succeed above all reasonable expectations. Then, look for ways to celebrate even modest improvements.

Robert Reed Church, Sr. was a millionaire business leader and philanthropist in Memphis, Tennessee. In 1865, his wife Louisa opened a string of beauty salons while Church acquired a saloon. Next, he added a restaurant and a downtown hotel to his holdings. During the race riots of 1866, a white mob shot him and left him for dead. Church recovered and vowed to remain in Memphis despite the anti-Black violence.

In 1899, Church used his own money to purchase a tract of land on Beale Street, where he built the country's first 2,000-seat music hall, recreational and cultural center. He employed W.C. Handy as their orchestra leader. Performers included the Fisk Jubilee Singers and speakers like Booker T. Washington. In 1902, President Theodore Roosevelt spoke to 10,000 people there.

Church was not alone; more than twenty other Blacks who were born slaves died as millionaires.

The majority of Black youths today are unaware of the vibrant spirit of entrepreneurship that prevailed throughout the Black community even during the most oppressive legalized segregation and racial discrimination. Few know about the strength of the Black trailblazers that survived and thrived throughout this oppressive era.

Free Blacks helped create Wilberforce University in Ohio in 1847. They created more than 100 private schools. In 1868, 1,000 Blacks were fired from the docks of Baltimore for striking for better wages. Then they organized and financed their own railroad, the Chesapeake Marine Dry Dock and Railroad Company, which operated from Baltimore to Maine for over 18 years.

When Blacks were denied access to inns and hotels, they built their own, the St. Charles in Chicago, the St. Theresa Hotel in New York City, and the Lord Calvert and Carver Hotels in

Miami. In Harlem, a real estate company in the 1930s employed more than 300 people.

People are inspired to improve their lives when they are given a vision of success, not by constantly reminding them of injuries to be avoided.

Success Springs from Motivation

There are two ways to prevent people from achieving and advancing themselves. The first is to prohibit them by law; the second is to convince them that it is useless to try because the deck is stacked against them.

That's why people should never be defined by circumstances beyond their control—a principle exemplified by the three women whose stories are popularized in the Oscar-nominated film "Hidden Figures."

Getting Personal

Based on a 2016 book by Margot Lee Shetterly, *Hidden Figures* chronicles how NASA mathematicians Mary Jackson, Katherine Johnson and Dorothy Vaughan overcame legal segregation and racial discrimination to play a critical role in astronaut John Glenn's orbital mission aboard Friendship 7 in 1962.

There is a thirst among Black Americans for such inspiring messages.

I witnessed evidence of this yearning when I attended a book signing with Ms. Shetterly at the Fredericksburg, Virginia, campus of the University of Mary Washington. The 1,000-seat auditorium was filled to capacity by a predominantly African-American audience. People were packed into the balcony, and there wasn't a spare inch of standing room anywhere along the walls.

The 100 copies of *Hidden Figures* that organizers had brought to the venue sold out well before the presentation began. Even the local bookstores ran out of copies.

During the question-and-answer session following Ms. Shetterly's talk, some in the audience lamented that they had not known earlier about the heroines of "Hidden Figures." Children in the audience excitedly raised their hands to learn more about these pioneering "human computers" and their triumph over adversity.

The women of *Hidden Figures* embodied this maxim. As Ms. Shetterly declared at her book-signing: "These are the kinds of stories that change your life. You see people doing these amazing things and you internalize it, you normalize it, and it completely changes your inner landscape and what you believe is possible."

Thousands of such stories are embedded in the history of Black America. Sadly, they are rarely told by the elite media—Black or white—and often ignored by academia.

Truly, the most powerful antidote to disrespect is not protest but performance. Stories that convey this idea, however, are considered "off message" in the national narrative. Instead Black youth are told that blame lies elsewhere.

Confronting "Race Grievance" and Affirmative Action

The dominant racial message today attributes Black failure—academic, occupational, and even moral—to an all-purpose invisible villain: "institutional racism." Those who shake their fists and proclaim that white America must change before Blacks can achieve anything are embracing a version of white supremacy clothed as protest.

The debilitating effects of this attitude are exacerbated by liberals' "white guilt." Since the time of "race norming" and the promotion of "Ebonics" as a separate national language in the 1960s, white liberals have approached the Black community with a combination of pity, patronage, and pandering.

Affirmative-action programs opened education and employment opportunities to a small group of privileged Blacks who were prepared to take advantage of them. But affirmative action did little to help the impoverished Black Americans who had served as the foot soldiers of the civil rights campaigns.

Today, the affirmative-action mentality permeates elite universities, where the arguments of Black "experts" are rarely challenged or debated by their white counterparts, and virtually never by their students. It's an academic environment in which every minority gets a trophy. And Blacks are re-segregating in the name of "equity."

Therefore, we disable people in two ways. **One is by denying them an opportunity to compete. The other, more crippling, is to tell them they no longer have to compete and that every door will be opened.** My heart goes out to those Black students who may never be confident that their degrees and accolades were the result of merit.

Black Americans must refuse to surrender to incompetence, self-devaluation, and self-marginalization of the "institutional racism" fallacy. Never before have all Americans had such opportunity. Success is theirs for the taking if they work for it.

Every day at my office, I pass a wall with a photograph of a group of slaves from 1861 titled "Strength." Under that picture is the inspiring quotation: "The strongest people in the world are not those most protected: They are the ones who must struggle against adversity and obstacles and surmount them to survive."

Woodson Principles in Action

With former Congressman and Secretary of Housing and Urban Development Jack Kemp's help, the Woodson Center held hearings to highlight grassroots leaders and neighborhood programs that are working, like the Cochran Gardens public housing in St. Louis, Missouri.

By changing housing rules, residents received the money that the housing authority was receiving, so that they could hire other residents. We saw drops in welfare dependency as well as dramatically reduced teen pregnancies, because the residents' indigenous leadership inspired people.

For three months, *60 Minutes* worked with us and did a show on resident-managed public housing, reporting these successes, focusing on inspiration. It is interesting, however, that not a single researcher on the left or the right of center has ever taken the time to find out why or how those places were succeeding or the implications for public policy.

If we want to know what works to reduce poverty in America, we must go into these islands of excellence that have been created by the people living there, try to find out what they have done that defies conventional wisdom, and then host conferences and conduct studies regarding the people who are successful.

We should be inspired by victories, not by people who have failed but people who have succeeded. Rather than always studying failure, we should ask, "What lessons can be learned from people suffering from the problem?"

Change by the Numbers

Researchers say 70 percent of those in poverty have been raised in dysfunctional homes. That means 30 percent have not!

Studying failure will reveal how to create failure. But if you want to know how to create success, we must go look for the successes.

That's why the Woodson Center goes into those 30 percent of the functioning households to locate the source of the knowledge and experience that is causing people to succeed and achieve in the midst of these toxic communities. Then we apply "Miracle-Grow" in terms of training and technical assistance, acting as venture capitalists.

By going in and applying resources and information that enables community leaders and residents to take what works among the 30 percent, we can apply it to the dysfunctional households and work to improve them.

One of our most famous grassroots leaders, Kimi Gray, was a divorced mother of five children on welfare, who lived in public housing. She got off welfare in three years and sent all five children to college. When word of her success got around, others asked for her help. A support group evolved and soon four other students from this neighborhood went off to college. When kids complained that they could not bring their friends home because of the dangerous and rundown condition of their housing complex, Kimi Gray and the residents took charge and became resident managers. Within ten years over 500 hundred kids went off to college. Teen pregnancy was nearly eliminated, the drug dealers were driven out of the complex and the community became peaceful.

Avoiding Obstacles and "Injuries"

Unfortunately, today unless evil wears a white face, it will avoid detection and be allowed to pursue its path of destruction with devastating consequences for those most in need of help. This is true about recent reports of widespread grade inflation and falsifying graduation criteria for Black children in the Washington, D.C., public school systems—which received just momentary mention in the news media and generated no public outrage.

When confronted with their schools' dismal records in student performance on standardized tests and embarrassingly low graduation rates, school officials chose to take the easiest route to secure their salaries and bonuses. They focused on tweaking the data in their reports, rather than investing in actually boosting the students' performance and class attendance.

Change by the Numbers

One of the most recent cases that emerged in the news was a graduation ceremony at D.C.'s Ballou High School, in which 50 percent of the students receiving diplomas had missed more than three months of school, and one in five had been absent more than they were present. Not surprisingly, in 2016, only nine percent of the school's students passed the English portion of the D.C. standardized test and literally not one student passed the math section.

When social-justice warriors talk about the school-to-prison pipeline, they are referring to an amorphous enemy of "institutional racism" that they say exists throughout the various institutions of society. But the real school-to-prison pipeline begins within various public-school systems, many of which are run by middle-class Blacks.

The rampant corruption and gross incompetence that is visited upon low-income Black children amounts to moral treason, and it is worthy of the level of public outrage that is directed at a racist flyer or a symbolic noose.

Healers and Heroes

In the winter of 1997, a twelve-year-old boy, Darryl Hall, was abducted and beaten by neighborhood rivals as he walked home from school. His body was discovered several days later in a nearby ravine. He had been shot, execution style, in the back of his head.

Four neighborhood leaders—James "Mac" Alsobrooks, Pete Jackson, Eric Johnson, and Arthur "Rico" Rush—could not be at peace unless they made some effort to prevent any retaliatory attack for Darryl's murder.

For days they walked the streets, talking to the young people to identify those who had influence in each of the warring factions. Their earnest pleas to the youth gradually won their trust, and representatives of each side agreed to meet in neutral territory—the offices of the Woodson Center in northwest D.C.

Suspicion and fear permeated the first closed-door meeting, which youth as young as twelve attended in bulletproof vests. Over the next two weeks, however, they came together several more times, and gradually began to open up. On January 30, they publicly declared a peace pact. As a result, crime in the neighborhood decreased dramatically.

In over twelve years there was just one recorded gang related murder in a community which previously had been notorious for its youth violence. A football field and playground that had been a deserted killing ground is now filled with the laughter of children. Residents declared that the neighborhood had not been alive like this since the sixties. The neighborhood mail carrier broke down in tears at the sight of kids who were formerly vicious enemies now joking and laughing together.

This peaceful intervention became the subject of a PBS television special.

The official who is currently functioning as a receiver for the District's Housing Department arranged to provide jobs for the young men refurbishing the neighborhood, removing graffiti, and landscaping. They eagerly seized the opportunity.

Plans are underway to provide additional training for the youth and to link them with counterparts in other areas of the country, former gang leaders who are now functioning as mentors for other youths in their communities.

Fundamental reform will mean changing our perspective, believing in the potential of the Black community, and capitalizing on the positive rather than the negative once and for all.

The writings of many of today's Black scholars have amounted to no less than a revisionist history of the Black community. This revised history focuses almost exclusively on the degradation whites have imposed on Blacks and the accomplishments of the civil rights leadership's efforts since the sixties.

Conveniently airbrushed from the portrait of Black America are the remarkable models of self-help—accomplishments of Black entrepreneurs and mutual aid societies even during eras of the most brutal racial repression and slavery.

Lost is the legacy—the inspiration—of personal responsibility and principle-based entrepreneurship that could provide today's youths with a pride in their heritage and an adaptable model that could guide their futures.

The selective history that is transmitted to our young people is, simply put, that Blacks came to this country on slave ships; from there they went to the plantations and slavery, from the plantations to the ghetto, and, finally, to welfare.

But a complete Black history would reveal that, even in the face of the most bitter oppression and bondage, many courageous Blacks persevered and accomplished, undaunted by the obstacles they faced.

Woodson Principles in Action

Kenilworth-Parkside was a classic example of a public housing program gone awry. The community was plagued with violent crime and drug trafficking and was rife with welfare dependency, teen pregnancy, and high school dropouts.

Kimi Gray led residents in this development to take on their properties' management duties. She recalls, "In 1983, housing authority leadership was uniformly opposed to any type of resident involvement. Although our development had no heat or hot water, Kenilworth-Parkside was always classified as a low priority for modernization."

When residents finally won management duties, they addressed the needs of the community as a whole. They began by establishing security patrols to oust drug dealers. Then they launched a college preparation program, "College Here We Come," through which nearly six hundred youths from the development were placed in college within a twelve-year period.

Within four years of resident management, welfare dependency was reduced by 50 percent, crime fell by 75 percent, and the rental receipts increased by 77 percent. A cost-benefit analysis conducted by an accounting firm projected that cost-efficient management by the residents would save the district government $4.5 million over a ten-year period.

The accomplishments of the residents at Kenilworth-Parkside were hard won. At one point, drug dealers who were angry about being evicted from their trafficking turf sabotaged the van that Gray used to transport her young students to their colleges, slashing the tires and filling the gas tank with dirt.

But the residents prevailed, setting up substance abuse centers, youth counseling, a day care center, and an on-site medical clinic. Their current focus involves a home-ownership project that would offer residents the opportunity to hold assets that could give them upward mobility.

Living "Above the Code"

Seven houses in Hollywood, Florida survived a major hurricane.

Only seven.

It turns out that they were all Habitat for Humanity houses. They were built "above the code" with additional braces in the roof, in the walls, in the windows. The houses and their owners prospered because they didn't do just what was required. They went above and beyond.

Grassroots leaders who engage in the restoration of men and women operate "above the code"; they strive to go beyond all reasonable expectations.

Like Kimi Gray, all the grassroots leaders in the Woodson Center's network began their outreach on the level of vision, values, and character. They often fulfill the role of a parent, providing not only authority and structure, but also the love that is necessary for an individual to undergo healing, growth, and development. Like a parent, their love is unconditional and resilient, and they are committed for the long haul. Most of them worked their own way out of poverty and into a healthy, contributing entity within our society. They begin their outreach with their own meager resources. They are committed for a lifetime.

That's why resident managers of housing projects and other grassroots leaders across the nation have succeeded in instances where the private sector and government initiatives have failed. The key to this extraordinary success is their firsthand knowledge of the problems, needs, and preferences of residents.

Help Others Become Extraordinary

As Dr. King said, the highest expression of maturity is the ability to be self-critical.

We need to come together as a nation to address the problems of poverty by empowering those at the bottom, giving them the opportunity to excel and participate in the free enterprise system. The most important component of this pursuit is inspiring others to revive the principles of self-determination, personal responsibility, vision, and values.

Juan Rivera lost seven years of his life to heroin addiction. His days were spent in burglaries to support his habit. His nights were lost in a haze of drugs. But back in 1972, the seeds were sown for a transformation in his life.

Today, he recalls a fateful morning when he was sitting, barebacked and shoeless, in front of his single-room shack. As a result of his addiction, his features were skeletal, his eyes hollow, and his hair was long and matted.

Juan lit his first cigarette and began thinking about what house he would burglarize that day. He shares that suddenly, "I found myself thinking on a deeper level, thinking about what I'd do with my life if I had another chance and about all the things I would have wanted to accomplish."

But then he stopped and caught himself, and remembered, "Once an addict, always an addict." He had tried and failed to escape his addiction before. He had changed his location, undergone therapy, and taken medication. He was convinced now that nothing would work.

Several months later, when he was at a court hearing, he met a man named Freddie Garcia, who told him that he was operating a program for addicts called Victory Home on the southwest side of San Antonio, Texas.

Freddie explained that he had once been an addict himself, and as he named some of the drug sources he had used, Juan recognized their street names and began to trust Freddie and to open up—until Freddie said that his addiction ended when he accepted Jesus Christ. Juan closed down. But he pocketed the card that Freddie had given him.

Months later, Juan was caught by the San Antonio police in a drug sweep. As Juan explains, most addicts treat a periodic lock-up as an occupational hazard:

> "Every drug addict knows that the best thing to do after a raid like that is just to lay back and take advantage of the wonderful generosity of taxpayers and look for a federally funded program. ... Addicts enter treatment, get on Methadone and, in return, entertain the psychiatrists and sociologists. The trick is to just play along with the system until all the pushers are

out of jail and reinstated on the streets. Then the addicts leave the treatment programs and the whole cycle starts over again."

Juan found Freddie's card and decided to use the program for his temporary stop-off. He put in a call and within fifteen minutes Freddie had arrived to pick him up.

Freddie's program draws addicts seeking to be freed from all across the country, and they have never turned anyone away. It is often so crowded that participants sleep in tents. Hardcore addicts who are suffering the ordeal of going "cold turkey" are given cots in a trailer. Dinners of rice and beans for more than a hundred people simmer in two big pots on the stove. But though the physical conditions of Victory Home are Spartan, it is rich in the compassion and love that make transformation possible.

Juan developed strong relationships with Freddie, his wife, Ninfa, and others at Victory Home. Ultimately, he overcame his addiction and has served there for more than 30 years as Freddie's right-hand man in this now-international ministry.

He shared:

> "I feel—not from arrogance but honesty—that today I could venture off into any profession, and I believe that I would be successful. Because I have learned how to live. And that is what sustains me. Freddie taught me through classroom instruction and through example. I learned how to live."

Beyond All Expectations

Throughout the past four decades, the Woodson Center has created a nationwide network of hundreds of Black, white, and brown grassroots leaders in low-income neighborhoods who have achieved remarkable victories in uplifting their communities and reclaiming lives.

Heroes and Healers

Kenilworth-Parkside community leader Kimi Gray shared the critical element of neighborhood transformation: self-determination. She described the results:

> Under resident management, we reduced crime, welfare dependency, recidivism, teen-age pregnancy, vandalism. We increased rent collections and setup businesses that employed residents. As the residents became confident in their ability to improve living conditions, they began seeking a more permanent stake in the future of the community. Homeowner-ship may have been what the Administration wants to do, but it was our dream also. Nobody talks about that.

Since the death of Dr. King, open and honest debate within the Black community has dwindled. As a consequence, even though the United States has spent trillions of dollars on anti-poverty programs, one-third of Black America is in danger of becoming a permanent underclass.

While this scenario has been a boon to middle- and upperclass Blacks who are employed within the government programs' bureaucracies and have entered the ranks of elected and appointed officials, conditions of low-income Blacks have continued to deteriorate.

So, if political empowerment, the passage of civil rights laws, and a proliferation of high price tag poverty programs have not yielded the promised benefits for those who are most in need, it's time for a revolution in the way we bring about change.

Poverty Is Not a Life Sentence

Those who are impoverished are not destined to a life of continued dependency but have the capacity to rise, if provided with support, guidance, and opportunity. Many of those who have redirected and reclaimed have transformed their character, but their "characteristics" or qualities remain and can be enlisted in service to their communities.

For example, former gang leaders maintain the respect and response among their peers that have enabled them to become powerful peer mentors and ambassadors for peace in their neighborhoods.

In my experience, inspiration is a critical part of real, lasting change. Committed community leaders who incorporate trust, reciprocity, and self-determination into relational treatment and healing become examples others can look up to and live by.

Woodson Principle #7

Inspiration

You can learn nothing from studying failure except how to create failure. Begin your inquiry by recognizing the capacity people possess. People are inspired to improve when they are presented with victories that are possible, not injuries to be avoided. Provide them with the tools for self-determination and help them strive to succeed above all reasonable expectations. Then, look for ways to celebrate even modest improvements.

Woodson Principle #8

Agency

No one should have to surrender his or her dignity as a condition for receiving help. Unconditional giving leads to pity rather than the desire to succeed. People should be agents of their own uplift. Never do more for them than they are willing to do for themselves. There must be reciprocity as the framework of any meaningful relationship. In other words, a person should be given the opportunity to give in return for what is received.

When I left high school at age 17 to join the Air Force, I came home after a year of being stationed in Florida. When it was time to return to base, I had already spent my car fare ahead of time, because I was so sure my mom, Anna, would give more to me.

She told me to get back the best way I could.

I hitchhiked a thousand miles, from Philadelphia to Cocoa Beach, Florida. It was rough. That incident helped to reinforce that my destiny is in my hands, that I can't rely on others to bail me out of my irresponsibility.

Entitlement: The Enemy of Agency

It is interesting, but largely unnoticed, that the recent college bribery scandal occurred at the same time that Democratic candidates for president were issuing statements supporting reparations to Blacks to compensate for slavery. There are striking similarities between what wealthy white parents are doing to injure their children with their supposed "help," and the potential injury that would be inflicted on Black youngsters who would be the supposed beneficiaries of reparations.

The scandal of buying one's child's way into college and the agenda of the race-grievance industry are two sides of one coin. The common denominator is that each begins with the premise that someone is entitled to something he or she otherwise might not earn. Everything goes downhill from there.

The youth share the notion that they are entitled to unearned benefits—either because their parents are rich and powerful, or because their parents are poor, Black, and powerless. The entitlement premise upon which these wealthy parents and the Democratic candidates engage with the larger society is detrimental to those they purport to help, and it undermines the values and norms of human interchange that can be built only on the foundation of meritocracy and concern for the content of our character.

First, treating people as if they are entitled teaches them the morally odious lesson that they do not have to work hard to achieve. Second, entitlement teaches the recipients to be uncertain or doubtful about their own real capacities. They never can tell when they go through a door whether it has been opened because of what they have done, or what their parents have done on their behalf. That robs them of the knowledge that they have agency and control over their lives.

Third, because there are no advances without setbacks, offering entitlement robs the recipients of the valuable lessons that failure teaches. We must master setbacks and disappointments; they create moral muscle, the foundation of good character.

Is it any wonder why children are growing up in America today without the capacity to withstand life's setbacks, large and small? When they lose a friend or get rejected in a love relationship, they are not equipped to handle it. That is part of the reason the suicide rate among wealthy youths is so high.

On the other side of the coin, consider how we treat low-income people, particularly low-income Blacks. Politicians point to the problems of low-income Blacks, from crime and violence to out-of-wedlock births and lack of economic opportunity. Their answer is reparations? This is condescending and cheap virtue-signaling for the purpose of garnering votes. The call for reparations presumes that something must be delivered to Blacks because on their own they have no agency.

If they do not exhibit agency, it is a consequence of the legacy of slavery or Jim Crow—in other words, any destructive behavior they exhibit is dismissed as not their own. "Don't blame the victim," the purveyors of entitlement declare.

This victim-mentality assumes Blacks are not in control, that their lives are defined by somebody the entitlement-peddlers say hates them and who must deliver the goods (reparations). "Until and unless white America gives you something, it's cruel to expect you to achieve on your own," they say.

This thinking, so prevalent today, ignores the fact that when racism was enshrined in law and visibly embedded in the culture, Black Americans achieved. Who today knows this history?

Like the books in Ray Bradbury's masterful novel *Fahrenheit 451*, it has been removed from the bookshelves of our collective memory. This history lays out the inconvenient fact that Blacks achieved against the odds under segregation. This achievement is not being taught today; you won't find books with such stories in the National Museum of African American History and Culture. The program of hobbling our young people with entitlements requires that those books cannot be found.

The merchants of racial grievance assume the same thing that upper-income white parents do about their kids: They assume young people have no agency.

Although different cases, the belief in entitlement that they share contributes to the destruction of a generation that is frightened of failure because they have been protected from it. In both cases, however, **the entitlement impulse amounts to attempting to give our children what we did not have, rather than what we did have—namely, the character to understand that real achievement must be earned.**

The "Racial Grievance" Industry

After the civil rights movement, Blacks were elected to office in unprecedented numbers. The "War on Poverty" enticed poor Blacks to sign up on the rolls of a steadily growing welfare system; assistance became a form of reparations to an entitlement-focused populace. Government programs and agencies took on the centrality that families, churches, and civic institutions once held.

Middle-class Blacks migrated into government jobs in record numbers as anti-poverty programs poured money into the cities in a dramatic expansion of the welfare system. Professional Blacks were stewards of that system. The goal was no longer to further progress made through self-determination but a pursuit of entitlements with a mentality of victimization.

In short, **self-degradation replaced self-determination.**

Today, the claim of the debilitating oppression of systemic racism is used as both a shield and a sword. It's a shield from blame for the failure of those entrusted with power to fulfill their responsibility and the trust that had been placed in them. It's a sword to attack a faceless external enemy that is presumed to determine the destiny of the Black community.

This is nothing short of a Black-authored version of white supremacy—an acceptance of impotence and victimhood, as if whites can somehow, by remote control, compel Blacks to act against their own interests.

Some of these new leaders believe that America cannot be redeemed and instead must be made to pay endless reparations and bear bottomless guilt for the transgressions she inflicted via slavery.

Reparations compensate the descendants of Black slaves who suffered at the hands of their white oppressors, who were able to build wealth and derive privileges that were passed on to their progeny. Advocates argue that it is the legacy of slavery that explains the current wealth gap between Blacks and whites in America and assume that the suffering of those early generations somehow can be monetized in a yet-to-be-determined amount.

By this reasoning, for the sake of social justice, all whites in America today must be willing to contribute to such a compensation fund or be labeled as racist. In this calculation, all Blacks living in America belong to the class of "aggrieved victims" and, therefore, qualify for reparations. Ultimately, the agenda of racial grievance has silenced the debate about goals and strategies for solutions that was vital to the civil rights movement.

A rising generation is being barraged with the message that the greatest stumbling block to their success is an amorphous, all-purpose villain of "institutional racism" and that, while any vestige of that remains, they cannot progress.

Yet, in our nation's largest cities, our children are failing in institutions and agencies under Black leadership and, in the absence of moral moorings and value-generating institutions, urban streets have become literal killing fields.

The "social justice warriors" have normalized failure for Black students, demanding that the bar of competency be lowered for their academic performance, attendance, and behavior. Ironically, their assumption that consistent standards should not be applied for all races also resonates with the message of white supremacy.

Heroes and Healers

Dr. Martin Luther King, Jr. believed that our nation's founders had set the nation on the right course and that racial groups must put aside their differences and acknowledge the principles that unite all Americans.

This is a far cry from today's race hustlers who profit handsomely in terms of money and power from keeping race a divisive front and center issue. They, along with their guilty white liberal enablers—and the media who cover both—pose as the vanguard of today's civil rights movement.

They cannot resist the opportunity to seize the podium or highly-visible positions in marches and protests before returning to their safe, upscale neighborhoods. They claim to represent the marginalized but bear no resemblance to either Dr. King or his methods.

Dr. King upheld the values of personal responsibility, reciprocity, and mutual support. It is on the foundation of those values and virtues that visionary Blacks in America were able to make great strides in business and education, even during pre-civil rights eras of the Reconstruction and Jim Crow.

For all groups, the road to recovery is through the power of redemption, not through racial grievance.

The Dangers of a Helping Hand

I think if you stopped a man on the street today and said, "How should we fight poverty in America?" he would say, "Well, there are all these things like food stamps and public housing, and that's how we fight poverty in America."

Then if we would ask, "How should we do more? How should we do it better?" he would say, "Well, we should spend more. We should reach more people who are in need."

It's like the default position is the welfare state. And the welfare state creates a path of least resistance.

During the Depression, President Roosevelt's emergency relief efforts created a professional class of social policy bureaucrats and a corps of sociologists, psychologists, and social workers who, in effect, formed a social service industry with its own social status, goals, and interests—a situation that often worked against the interests of the poor.

This governmentknows-best policy herded low-income families into high-rise buildings that bred crime and frustration, discouraged the work ethic, fostered dependency on public assistance, and stifled the initiative of small entrepreneurs with programmedto-fail bureaucratic restrictions.

In 1964, the same year that the landmark Civil Rights Act was passed, a host of anti-poverty programs were also spawned, including food stamp legislation, the Economic Opportunity Act (which was the cornerstone of the War on Poverty), and programs for mass transportation.

On the heels of this legislation, in 1965, additional legislation included Medicare and Medicaid, the Elementary and Secondary Education Act, the Higher Education Act, and the Public Works and Economic Development Act.

In essence, the poverty programs were advertised as the means of fulfilling the civil rights promise in a nation burdened by the guilt of a history of racial discrimination. However, like the misdirected civil rights agenda, the programs and policies of the poverty industry are embraced on the basis of their purported intent alone, without regard to their success or failure in achieving their purpose. Powerful economic interests which derive their legitimacy from the civil rights establishment have now calcified around old racial wounds.

While only two out of ten college-educated whites now work for the government, as many as six out of ten Blacks with college educations hold government jobs—the majority with the social service industry or with the education system. Because the careers of these service providers are ensured by a client base of the poor who are dependent on them, the self-sufficiency of low-income Blacks poses a threat to their guardians in the poverty industry.

A condition now exists where the interests of one group of Blacks is in direct conflict with the interests of another.

Expert Opinion

At the turn of the century, Booker T. Washington presciently warned against the agenda of those "problem profiteers," proclaiming:

> *"There is a class of colored people who make a business of keeping the troubles, the wrongs, and the hardships of the Negro race before the public. Having learned that they are able to make a living out of their troubles, they have grown into the settled habit of advertising their wrongs—partly because they want sympathy, and partly because it pays. Some of these people do not want the Negro to lose his grievances, because they do not want to lose their jobs."*

Can you imagine that the reason that there's such resistance to people changing these entitlement programs is that 70 percent of every dollar we spend on the poor doesn't go to them?

It goes to those who serve the poor. They have morphed into a poverty industry, in which the poor have become a commodity.

Federal and state governments currently provide more than eighty programs that provide cash, food, housing, medical service, and more to poor and low-income Americans. That price tag is over a trillion dollars a year…and the percentage of people receiving government assistance has now outpaced the percentage of Americans who do not.

These programs have not worked. The poor, in even greater numbers, are still with us. A permanent underclass of more than one-third of all Black Americans, unskilled and undereducated, remains untouched by civil rights gains, the War on Poverty, increased Black political power, and a mammoth social welfare industry.

An alarmingly high number of Blacks have developed a welfare dependency on government programs that, while providing a bare minimum cash source, both subsidizes poverty and saps individual initiative.

Ultimately, we must encourage the briefest possible time on public assistance, because the goal is to have people move off of these programs, not live on them.

Reciprocity and Regeneration

Helping an individual…even a whole community…can never be about charity. We're not intervening to rescue someone from themselves or from circumstances beyond their control. Instead, the right expectation is that **no one should do more for someone than they are willing to do for themselves.**

Presented from another angle, a true act of compassion does not require the surrender of self-respect in exchange for assistance. The principle of reciprocity should guide the philanthropic exchange just as it guides exchange in the marketplace.

People who are constantly on the receiving end, who have never been given the opportunity to reciprocate, will in due time despise not only the gift, but also the gift giver.

That's why truly effective grassroots leaders and healers always contain an essential element of reciprocity…they require and demand a return on their investment from the people they assist.

For example, the Woodson Center works with communities and organizations to offer summer camps for kids in low-income areas. But the camps are never "free." Every child and teen must earn the right to come, whether they participate in community cleanup, taking the elderly to the grocery store, or something else…anything that will foster a sense of self-worth and pride.

If the forces of "effective compassion" and volunteerism do not move beyond the notion of "rescue" from the outside, and if they do not channel their support and seek guidance from indigenous community institutions, they will simply create passive recipients who make good clients but poor citizens.

Regardless of the sincerity and personal quality of their compassion, they will, likewise, injure with the helping hand.

Woodson Principles in Action

The director of a shelter for battered women in a small mountain town held a Christmas celebration at a home for battered women.

As Christmas approached, toys and clothing donated by local businesses began to arrive at the shelter. Volunteers wrapped and tagged the gifts for the children and placed them beneath the tree.

On the day of the event, the director stood in the back of the room and watched the presentation of the Christmas gifts. She saw that the donors were beaming. The volunteers and staff were smiling. Yet that same joy did not seem to emanate from the mothers who stood by or even from their children who were opening their gifts.

The director realized that the problem was not the gifts, which ranged from Barbie dolls to bicycles, but the fact that the mothers did not feel that they had contributed to the event and had no input regarding the gifts their children received.

The next year, she planned the Christmas party very differently. Months before the holiday, the staff drew up lists of tasks, from cooking and cleaning to clerical work. Residents of the shelter who took on different tasks were paid with special vouchers. The gifts that were donated that year were displayed on shelves at the shelter's "gift store."

Just before Christmas, the women took their vouchers and went shopping for presents for their children. The gifts the children received that year brought them more joy than ever before: each present was an expression of a mother's love and investment.

This model can be used to guide all efforts to support and uplift low-income individuals and communities. Outreach to those in need should always be offered in a way that recognizes and builds on the capacities of its recipients.

Solving poverty is not about systems, delivery, program, or service. It's about individual human beings who have complex needs and live in complex circumstances. That's what makes public policy so difficult to create and orchestrate.

Confronting Competing Interests

In order for the Black self-help movement to flourish and prosper, several impediments must be confronted and changed. Many people who say they are social justice warriors actually patronize and demean the poor by assuming that they cannot survive without external help.

On the other hand, those caught in poverty can become so caught up in seeking welfare state handouts that they lose their own souls. The very important, but essentially private, matter of what indignities ancestors suffered because of their race must not be allowed to become a vehicle for cheap brokering with the welfare state.

The generations of Blacks who suffered under Jim Crow deserve something more than simply having their travails used as an excuse for current failures. Past sufferings should not be hauled out to gain guilt money. Such a posture is pitiful and unbecoming of Black America's proud heritage.

Dependency, even when one is dependent on sympathetic and generous souls, is destructive of dignity.

Expert Opinion

We must ask, what is the character of public assistance, and does the character and the culture formed by those programs help or hurt relationships?

—Jennifer Marshall,
The Heritage Foundation

Undoing the Damage of Welfare

Throughout the nation as a whole, forty percent of children are born to single mothers; in the Black community, the incidence of births outside of marriage has skyrocketed to more than seventy percent.

Lest the blame for these dismal statistics be assigned to the catch-all culprit currently in vogue—institutional racism—a look to data on the family in the Black community in an era of legalized segregation and racial discrimination reveals that in 1960 nearly eighty percent of Black children lived in homes with both a mother and father. The proportion of Blacks aged 25 and older who had never married was just nine percent in 1960, compared with nearly forty percent today.

The tragic plummet of marriage and family throughout Black America since the mid-1960s is due largely to the creation of a self-perpetuating welfare system that was marked by disincentives and penalties for a key stepping stone to self-sufficiency: entering a marital union.

This devastating flaw might have been unintentional in some quarters, but it was part of a calculated strategy of some of the academic elite who announced a goal of crushing the establishment with the unsustainable weight of the welfare rolls and who accepted the demise of the Black family as collateral damage in this agenda.

In reality, removing stifling restrictions from marriage in the welfare system could help slow the family dissolution that has been going on throughout the past fifty years, but still more must be done to restore marriage and the family.

A person should never have to surrender their dignity as a price of being helped. They always have at least some capacity to help themselves. They have something important to contribute. And it's our job to help discover what that is…not suppress it in service of another agenda.

The Political Chasm and Poverty

On both the left and the right, those who have dominated the policy arena share one trait in common: They are locked in a "program" mentality that is averse to innovation and thinking "outside the box." Debates amount to no more than tinkering within the system.

One side sees the ineffectiveness of the welfare system as evidence of the need to cut spending, while the other side uses stagnant poverty as proof that programs must be expanded. In sum, liberals believe the pathway out of poverty is lined with benefits, while conservatives think the poor can be starved into self-sufficiency.

Meanwhile, the poor are trapped in a virtual laboratory maze in which, through material incentives or disincentives, the "cheese" is moved around to direct the path they take.

On the extremely rare occasion when a major conservative political figure evidences any concern at all for the poor, it's not long before he or she stumbles into some clumsy or awkward formulation, prompting a massive counterstrike from the gate-keepers of poverty programs. The conservative beats a hasty retreat back to the safety of his or her ideological lines, muttering, "There's no votes there anyway—remind me again why I even raised this issue in the first place?"

And so the issue of poverty settles back once again into its accepted place, ignored by chastened conservatives and exploited by liberals confident that they still hold the moral high ground. The former propose no solutions, and the latter propose government solutions that are wildly improbable and expensive, reflected in proposed federal budgets that even the Democratic leadership doesn't take seriously.

Heroes and Healers

When Representative Paul Ryan approached me in the waning days of the presidential election of 2012, my first, admittedly uncharitable, thought was, "Oh yes, the Republican whiz kids just woke up to the fact that there aren't enough white people in America anymore to elect Mitt Romney. So, they're coming to one of the few Black activists who will even return their calls to see if they can't scrounge up some Black votes."

I speak from experience—that has happened before, and after a fleeting moment of interest in the Woodson Center and the problems of low-income people, conservative leaders typically move on to issues that mobilize their base, rather than trying to reach beyond it.

But from our first trip together to Cleveland to visit groups that are working successfully to solve the problems of poverty, I knew that Paul was different.

He didn't come with me to lecture the poor about their moral depravity. That's more easily done in the secure and tastefully decorated lecture halls of Washington's think tanks. Instead, Paul sat for hours with individuals emerging from poverty and heard stories of how they did it, what worked for them to break the bonds of addiction or family tragedy or unemployment.

Yes, government programs had often supported them in time of need, and some government funding was coming to the groups that had helped them, along with private charity. Paul didn't hear denunciations of federal programs that are bloated and expensive, because many of them aren't; many of them work well and deserve continued support.

But he also heard that those programs could be helpful only after individuals had made the deeply personal choice to make fruitful use of the services offered. That meant first a profound change of heart, a decision to take charge of their own lives, often with the help of grassroots groups that were in turn taking charge of their own neighborhoods.

There was nothing demeaning, defeatist, or depraved in the stories he heard. They were stories of responsibility, redemption, and resurrection. They were stories of individuals who were able to lift themselves out of lives that—contrary to stereotypes—no one would choose to live, through a recovery of moral character that—contrary to liberal stereotypes—is not "blaming the victim" but empowering individuals to begin the climb out of poverty.

In short, they were stories of profound hope, not passive despair.

Paul shared some of what he experienced with other Congress members and constituents...opening a critical conversation about how to provide effective, long-term solutions to poverty.

Breaking Free from Good Intentions

Too often, the disadvantaged are victims of "injury by the helping hand." Assistance offered by those who have a "rescuer from the outside" mentality, ignores and denies the capacities that exist among those they serve.

People who are now "protected" by government aid programs need to be empowered by them. Policies should be geared toward maximizing independence, economic opportunity, and freedom of choice for those receiving government funded services. **Regulatory and procedural barriers that prevent a community from starting its own schools, day care centers, and adoption agencies, must be removed.**

It is time to approach the needs of the Black underclass from a different perspective, one that is cognizant of the existing strengths within the Black community; one that recognizes the abilities and ingenuity of individuals and groups in handling their own affairs; and one that keeps government intervention to a minimum.

Regardless of their educational backgrounds, those experiencing the problems of poverty must play a primary role in developing avenues of escape. Above all, the Black community must disentangle itself from the welfare professionals whose primary objective has become the maintenance of clients.

Those who purport to serve the poor must be held accountable and must offer realistic programs that will inspire self-help to alleviate the conditions of the underclass. **The ultimate goal, after all, is economic independence and self-sufficiency…to build a commitment to agency.**

Woodson Principle #8

Agency

No one should have to surrender his or her dignity as a condition for receiving help. Unconditional giving leads to pity rather than the desire to succeed. People should be agents of their own uplift. Never do more for them than they are willing to do for themselves. There must be reciprocity as the framework of any meaningful relationship. In other words, a person should be given the opportunity to give in return for what is received.

WOODSON PRINCIPLE #9

Access

Eliminate barriers to access and serve all who suffer. Support positive incremental change through flexible options, not directives. Always strive to be "on tap and not on top." Expectations in the absence of opportunity are restrictive. People must be given the tools to take advantage of the opportunities presented to them.

Right out of college, I became a social worker. I was so determined to see change…so determined to help kids…so determined to make a difference. I was shocked by the constraints placed upon me by our inflexible foster care system. It broke my heart. Still does.

One particular situation sticks out in my mind. When we would have to remove kids from a house, we would always buy them some clothes and shoes before taking them to a foster home. That way they would have what they need before going to school and such.

But then, when I would move kids from a foster home back to their family home, regulations were in place that prevented us from buying them clothes, even if I had done so out of my own pocket. A year later, they had outgrown everything, and the soles of their shoes were just flapping as they walked. Even then, the system wouldn't flex to care for their needs.

I could not use common sense in helping these mothers whose children had been in foster care because the rules are rigged against them. For example, the agency was willing to pay the cost of removing the children when it would have been cheaper to take a small amount of money to pay a babysitter so the mother could go grocery shopping instead of leaving her twelve-year-old to babysit. This was a common reason kids were taken into placement. The agency is motivated to retain children in their care because that's how their professional salaries are paid; they are disincentivized to reunite children with their parents.

One day, I couldn't stand it anymore. I was taking this precious child back to his home after months in foster care. He didn't have a thing besides the old sweatshirt and ripped jeans he was wearing.

I took him to the store and bought him a few sets of new clothes and a pair of shoes. And I can't even tell you the amount of trouble I got into from my bosses!

I learned a very important lesson that day, and it has shaped my work ever since: **Inflexible policy can prevent us from exercising compassion and can run directly against common sense. We must eliminate barriers to access and serve all who suffer.**

The Dangers of Generalization

We cannot generalize about those who are struggling in poverty.

Through my experience with the Woodson Center and the nearly 3,000 community groups working in low-income neighborhoods that we have served, I have come to understand that all people are not poor for the same reason. It follows that our remedies must be as diverse as the reasons why particular populations are in poverty.

I have identified four categories of poor people. Category One includes those whose character is intact, but who have no money because they have lost a job, experienced a catastrophic financial event, or a breadwinner has passed away. For these people, the welfare system can function as it was originally intended—providing temporary support until recipients can find their footing again.

Category Two is comprised of those who remain dependent on the welfare system because the disincentives to marriage and work are embedded in its regulations, making it a rational choice to avoid self-sufficiency. In sum, they've "done the math" and realized it's not worth the loss of benefits to take the first steps toward upward mobility.

ROBERT L. WOODSON, SR.

In Category Three, people are disabled and need help. They cannot and will not be able to provide for their own needs without aid. Unfortunately, even in the disabled population, some people will discourage their children from learning or achieving because they will lose a Supplemental Security Income (SSI) check.

Finally, those in Category Four are individuals who suffer with character deficits that drive them to take chances and make choices that keep them impoverished—for example, those who are living with the consequences of alcoholism and addiction. These are the people that, given money and services, are injured by a helping hand.

Success Depends on Variety

First of all, the failure to develop an effective agenda is rooted in a misdiagnosis of the problem of poverty. People on the left tend to look at all poor people as if they fall into Category One, while people on the right tend to look at all poor people as if they fall into Category Four.

Even among those who have the best intentions, policy-makers on the left and right are deadlocked in debates about solutions, because we are addressing entirely different cohorts of the poor.

The people in Categories One and Two use the welfare system in the way it was intended, as an ambulance service, not a transportation system. They receive help, but then they move on, eventually climbing out of poverty to self-sufficiency. Applying the same remedies to Category Four, however, is disabling to those people. They do not have the will, desire, or motivation to achieve...and the welfare system allows them to remain in poverty for a lifetime.

It is not surprising that, with regard to those in Category Two, there has been no rush to reform a system that has trapped thousands in dependency or to promote their move toward self-sufficiency. The welfare system has swelled to comprise hundreds of different programs. States are rewarded for the numbers on its welfare rolls rather than those it has helped rise from dependency, and a bloated bureaucracy absorbs seventy cents of every dollar designated to address poverty.

The facts are incontestable: After the expenditure of over $20 trillion in a fifty-year "War on Poverty," the number of impoverished Americans has barely budged. The obvious failure of the "one size fits all" strategy that has dominated our nation's antipoverty agenda is testament to a critical need to reassess the fundamental assumptions that have guided policies.

Reform is vital—not only to stop the waste of what is now an annual expenditure of almost $1 trillion on an ineffective plan, but, more importantly, for the sake of millions of Americans and generations of families who are spending years in demeaning dependency.

In short, poverty has become an industry and its commodity is the ranks of its dependents.

Expert Opinion

Martin Luther King did not win justice; he won freedom. Justice-focused groups today, like Black Lives Matter, keep casting minorities as victims of America's old injustices, the better to work white guilt—to extract payoff of some kind. But Blacks make little to no progress and, worse, the preoccupation with injustice only leaves them eternally inconsolable and cut off from their own best energies and talents.

Suppose American conservatism begins to argue for progress as the best way to overcome inequality—not to the exclusion of justice, but simply as America's guiding light in social reform. Progress is accessible, possible, measurable and most of all doable.

To put all this on a dangerously romantic level: Why not go back to that perpetually workable thing, the American dream?

—Shelby Steele, Senior Fellow,
The Hoover Institution

With regard to Category Four, giving "no-strings attached" aid to those whose poverty is due to the chances they take and the choices they make simply enables them to continue their self-destructive lifestyles—in essence, injuring with the helping hand.

For this group, a fundamental revitalization in vision, character, and values is a prerequisite for them to reclaim their lives and escape from dependence. Until that is achieved, no amount of cash payments or benefits can engender a change in their circumstances.

However, a better life has always been available to those who reject undisciplined and irresponsible behavior and embrace self-determination and personal responsibility.

Positive Change Through Flexible Options

Grassroots leaders embrace the need for flexibility and access while addressing the needs of the poor, providing options along the way to self-sufficiency.

They know that every person cannot be reached in exactly the same way. Even where there may be a pervasive theology or philosophy in a program, not every person is expected to embrace it or be affected by it in the same way.

Their programs are open to all comers. The grassroots leaders do not target their services exclusively to individuals of any particular race or background. **Help is offered, instead, on the basis of the need a person has and his or her desire to change.**

The Woodson Center's nationwide network of community leaders and organizations includes John Ponder's HOPE for Prisoners. He founded this Las Vegas-based organization to facilitate the reentry of men and women who are leaving incarceration or some aspect of the judicial system.

They help individuals create and execute a personal plan to develop the relationships and skills that they need to reintegrate successfully into their homes, the workplace, and the community.

John Ponder's life is a testimony to the transforming power of God, and he is now helping to transform the lives of others.

From his personal saga of spending years in and out of prison, John understood firsthand the gravitational pull of his old lifestyle and predatory behavior, in the absence of a counterforce of support, opportunity and a vision for the future.

When he was empowered to reclaim and redirect his life through a series of compassionate, dedicated mentors, he dedicated himself to helping others to do the same.

John understood that the lack of opportunity to work and be a productive citizen was not the reason that most people went to prison in the first place. Merely providing access to opportunity upon their release from prison would not be enough to put them on the path to personal responsibility.

Internment does not affect all offenders in the same way or to the same degree. For those who have changed their attitude and taken responsibility for their crimes during incarceration, access to external resources such as job training, educational programs, and employment opportunities may be sufficient for their successful reentry into society and their families.

Tragically, for the majority of men and women returning from imprisonment, opportunity alone is not enough. They face internal barriers of attitude, absence of vision and trust, and carry with them the mentality of the self-centered criminal lifestyle.

Many entered a life of crime and imprisonment in a wounded and broken state. Others suffered abuse and abandonment in their lives. Research has shown that up to seventy percent of people in our nation's prison spent time in foster care, experiencing a series of placements and disruptions in their living situations, each of which may have damaged their socioemotional development and well-being.

For men and women who carry with them these obstacles upon release from prison, successful reentry and the prospect for becoming productive members of their community will require committed intervention and preparation to address character development and personal transformation.

That's why HOPE for Prisoners is dedicated to instilling in participants the hope, trust, and vision needed to begin the process of individual, internal redemption through the personal investment and guidance of mentors.

The most powerful—and surprising—group of mentors are officers of the Las Vegas Metropolitan Police Department. In many cases, these are the officers who initially arrested these men and women years ago!

As they guide their mentees through life-skills and job-readiness training and help them to reestablish family relationships, the officers create heartfelt, transparent relationships with them. Both the police officers and former offenders undergo a transformation in the way in which they see one another…and approach others who are struggling with the same issues.

John shared, "Not only do we men and women view law enforcement from a different perspective, but on the other side of the equation, it's helping law enforcement begin to look at the men and women who are coming home from prison, who are truly fighting for a second chance, from a whole different lens."

Change by the Numbers

To date, national rates of prison recidivism have been dismal. According to the Bureau of Justice Statistics, 68 percent of those released from prison were rearrested within three years, 79 percent within six years, and 83 percent within nine years.

In contrast, more than 2,300 men and women have graduated from HOPE for Prisoners, many of whom have begun to guide others. A University of Nevada, Las Vegas evaluation of the program discovered that over 64 percent found stable employment; only six percent were reincarcerated.

Yet the most powerful evidence of the transforming power of the program are the stories of its participants—they learn to support themselves and their families and transform from people who were takers to people who desire to give back. They achieve the self-sufficiency we dream of for every American.

Eliminate Obstacles for Those Who Need Help

Sixty percent of kids who become trapped in sex trafficking come from the foster care system; seventy percent of people in prison have spent time in foster care as well. Eighty percent become homeless…and less than twenty percent ever live above the poverty line.

I have witnessed firsthand how insidiously policy becomes a serious barrier to positive outcomes. The foster care system destroys children and families with its "helping hand."

For more than fifty years, the foster care system has treated children entrusted to its care as a commodity. Once a child is legally declared a ward of the state, there is resistance to reuniting the child with his or her parent(s) or finding an adoptive family. Decades ago, as a young social worker in a small town near Philadelphia, I witnessed this "foster care trap."

One mother facing hard times followed the advice of her caseworker and voluntarily committed her three children to temporary placement. After six months, she had secured a job and requested the return of her children. The agency assessed the living conditions in her home, and then said she needed an additional bedroom. There were other requirements, and the financial cost of compliance was beyond her means. Her bitterness about the situation confirmed to the caseworker that she should not care for her children.

They were never returned to her care.

In another case, agency representatives found a 12-year-old babysitting his younger siblings while his mother shopped for groceries. She was given a warning but when this happened again, the children were removed from the home. The agency would not provide the mother with money for a babysitter, and they required her to visit her children in their foster home 20 miles away, even though she did not have a car, or risk the permanent termination of her parental rights.

In each of these instances, the agency collected $15,000 annually for each child in reimbursements from the state.

Following rigid policy in practice defeated the original good intentions with which it was designed…and our nation's children are paying the price.

Woodson Principles in Action

Safe Families is a foster care agency with a completely unique approach. They believe—and I with them—that rebuilding families one-by-one is the ultimate key to pulling children up and out of the system and giving them a real opportunity for a successful life.

They are accredited by the foster care system, so they can work within the bounds of policy directives while removing the barriers to positive outcomes.

Safe Families always works from within the church, pairing a hurting family with a host family. Sometimes a family coach even moves into a troubled home, doing things as simple as driving the kids to school or teaching them good hygiene.

When children are taken into foster care, church families mobilize around both the foster family and the biological family. They coordinate with one another to create an individualized plan to provide care and reunite the family. Ultimately, the goal is to move the entire family to a point of healthy self-sufficiency.

Within the next five years, the Woodson Center and Safe Families have set a goal to reduce the number of kids in foster care in the areas they serve by fifty percent!

It is time for a new and bold strategy. The Woodson Center plans to assemble a consortium of groups that are applying innovative approaches to rescuing children from the foster care system by identifying best practices and bringing them together from a five-state area to develop joint interventions. The goal is to reduce the foster care population by fifty percent in three years. Armed with this experience we would then apply it to the entire country. It would be a combination of preventing children from coming into the system, such as Safe Families seeks to do, to increase adoptions as Harvest of Hope does, and a range of other interventions.

"Villains" and "Victims" No More

Social conflict is all the rage today. Careers are ended based on accusations of something said or done decades ago. Truth is increasingly in the eye of the beholder. That's why I believe it is more important than ever to be radically objective. And when the lines are drawn between villain and victim, we are required to be even more objective in our assessment of the situation and the solutions we choose.

The yearly March of Remembrance from Selma to Montgomery, Alabama, winds its way for forty-three miles through Lowndes County, one of the poorest Black rural communities in the country. Living conditions there have become much worse than they were back in the 1960s. Civil Rights groups pay little attention to the desperate needs of the people, even as they celebrate history and protest the present.

Local and state governments have sought to remedy this by electing Blacks to public office. Mayors, county commissioners, and school boards are all dominated by Black leaders, yet the social and economic decline over the decades has continued unabated.

Many of these local officials have the passion and commitment to help their people but lack the experience and knowledge to know what to request from the government or potential private sector providers. They don't know where to turn for help, much less what help is available.

I learned about the issue when Catherine Flowers called the Woodson Center for an appointment and came in with a group of ten elected public officials from around the county. The group originally came to Washington to attend the annual celebration of the Congressional Black Caucus. They sought help from their elected congressional representative, but all he offered were free tickets to an annual boat ride down the Potomac.

When they arrived, she asked for our help to address a specific crisis. Twenty homeowners were threatened with jail and evictions from their trailer homes due to unsafe septic systems. They were also struggling with inordinately expensive electric power bills, some of which exceeded the cost of residents' monthly mortgages.

Catherine and her group persuaded me to come and take a look. What started out as a one-day investigative visit became five years of intense involvement with the citizens of Lowndes County.

Together, we identified grassroots leaders, the Josephs, and we raised over $5 million from area pharaohs. Next, we established a field office managed by Mrs. Flowers that produced major improvements throughout the county. But it all began with preventing the jailing of those twenty homeowners and finding solutions to the high cost of their electric power bills.

From the beginning, state officials and representatives of the power company assumed we would come in to identify them as the villain and the homeowner as the victims. Instead, we sought detailed information about the Health Department's requirements for correcting damaged septic tanks, identified someone to fix them, and found the money to pay for it.

When a repair plan was presented to the state officials and the courts, all legal action was suspended and the homeowners were given more time. This solved the short-term problem. We used the same practical problem-solving to address the high cost of power bills. The Woodson Center brought in an engineer to conduct an assessment. His report enabled all parties to understand what the residents were doing to contribute to their problem and what concessions were made by the power company.

In the end, taking away the "villain" and "victim" labels helped create harmony, cooperation, and positive relationships that worked to the benefit of all parties.

WOODSON PRINCIPLE #10

Grace

Love and respect others, even when it's inconvenient. Look at neighborhoods as filled with people who have potential, not dysfunctional victims. The foundation of grace is radical forgiveness; a refusal to be held back by what used to be a hindrance in your life, real or imagined. Be free of bitterness, regret, and uncertainty about the future.

My heart is breaking over the rich legacy of the civil rights movement being pilfered and misappropriated by identity groups in their quest for power and influence. They are aided by a parade of Black scholars and pundits who publish books that focus on the history of slavery, Jim Crow and other past oppressions, and attribute present-day dysfunction among Blacks to the persistence of this racist legacy.

As a veteran of the civil rights movement, I remember how our most effective weapon against bigotry, hatred and oppression is *radical grace*. If social activists want to mimic us, let them follow in this direction rather than demand the elevation of their particular interests above all others.

Most activists focus on group identity. Past wrongs fuel anger and resentment, deepening divisions instead of erasing them. The only antidote to the growing conflict is for Black America to take back its historical victories against injustice from those repurposing them as ammunition for an anti-American agenda.

If income class, gender, or racism were the root causes of societal disintegration, then why do we find the same widespread self-destruction occurring across all of our society?

Middle school teacher Stephen Paddock fired more than a thousand rounds of ammunition from a Las Vegas hotel suite into a group of concertgoers, killing fifty-eight people and leaving hundreds injured.

Erik and Lyle Menendez gunned down their parents in a cold-blooded, premeditated act of murder as they watched television in their affluent suburban home.

Drug overdoses killed 63,632 Americans in 2016, crossing the lines of socioeconomic class more evenly than ever before.

Our white, upper-income society is facing the same heartbreaking violence, rising suicide rate, and increasing substance abuse as our nation's low-income minority neighborhoods. That means Black and other minority communities cannot place their hope for survival in demands for an end to racism and economic disparity.

All of this pain and brokenness comes from a common origin: our search for meaning. We crave purpose...belonging...respect.

We *need* grace, real love, and mercy that are neither earned nor deserved.

Notice that economic class, race, and gender have nothing to do with these basic needs. It's all about who we are as people, what we want for our lives, and who we hope to become.

So what does that mean for poverty alleviation? For taking care of the thousands of foster children in our society? For bringing hope from inner-city neighborhoods to the halls of Congress?

We start by believing the truth: that we are all chasing the same thing...true meaning for our lives. And then we grant each other grace.

Heroes and Healers

In 1962, during the early days of the civil rights movement, the Rev. Charles Billups, a Korean War veteran and a leading crusader in Alabama, and two of his Black coworkers were dragged into cars when they left their night shift. Billups was chained to a tree and savagely beaten.

The four Klansmen who attacked him placed a hot branding iron on Billups's stomach that left the letters "KKK" as a permanent scar. Later, one of the assailants became remorseful and came to Billups's home offering to turn himself in. Instead of demanding retribution, Billups declined to press charges and prayed with his attacker.

Robert Smalls was born into slavery in 1839 in Beaufort, South Carolina. During the Civil War in 1862, he and other dockworker slaves commandeered a Confederate supply ship, picked up their families along with other slaves, and safely steered the ship past five Confederate forts. Congress honored Smalls and awarded him $1,500 for seizing enemy assets.

He went on to become a successful businessman and member of Congress during Reconstruction, and he eventually purchased the plantation in South Carolina where he had been a slave.

In an act of grace, he took in and cared for family of his former owners, who had become destitute.

None of those people deserved the forgiveness they received, but by reconciling with them anyway, men like Smalls and Billups shrank the divide between their warring communities. The divisions that would normally keep people apart disappear in a celebration of forgiveness. They know they are the recipients of grace and take seriously the second chance.

This is a model for anyone seriously interested in erasing injustice and promoting equality. Nobody grows when activists are intolerant of others' flaws or demand the end of careers because of past wrongs. Emphasizing past evil—let alone manufacturing racial attacks to satiate the media's appetite—inflames anger on both sides.

Let us wisely choose grace instead.

Build Strong Alliances

An active, beneficial partnership between the Josephs of our nation's low-income communities and our modern-day pharaohs requires nothing short of a fundamental paradigm shift—an essential change in the assumptions that have guided the relationships between individuals with resources and individuals in need of support.

We can no longer look at this relationship as one between donors and recipients. Charity is not the model for the interchange between our nation's pharaohs and Josephs. In the Old Testament, the Pharaoh did not approach Joseph with charity. His goal was not to establish a welfare system for the people of Egypt or food stamps for Joseph's people.

No, he said, "Let us come together to address this danger or it will consume us all."

Like their biblical counterpart, although today's Josephs deserve to be heeded by modern-day pharaohs—political leaders and leaders of the business community—their effectiveness is not dependent on such recognition. Long before support or acknowledgment came from the outside, the Josephs of our nation lived committed lives of service and accomplished miraculous changes in the lives of those they served.

An alliance based on mutual recognition of each other's roles and abilities will allow today's Josephs and pharaohs to expand and further develop their transforming efforts for the benefit of our entire nation.

That's my motivation for starting the Woodson Center. We begin by convincing the American public that when it comes to poverty alleviation, when it comes to all the problems of moral decline, homelessness, violence, and suicide, everything has a common origin. We are all searching for meaning and purpose in our lives.

When that's missing, when life seems hopeless and meaningless, that's when we revert to the self-destructive behavior.

The same holds true in inner-city neighborhoods and wealthy suburbs.

What my grassroots leaders—and via their support, my funders and government leaders—do, is act. They give others opportunities to find a common purpose, and then they bear witness to the fact that when God helps you to understand that purpose, you can overcome all kinds of difficulties.

And if my grassroots leaders can rebuild their lives in these high-crime, drug-infested, toxic neighborhoods, if they can find meaning in the midst of all this chaos, then they have much to teach the sons and daughters of people who are trapped in these "gilded ghettos" of wealth and education.

The heart of the Woodson Center serves as a meeting place for those who have witnessed that transformation and redemption are possible. **God uses people. Broken people. Average people. The people you'd never expect. And He does big things.**

Getting Personal

I remember testifying before the Senate with two psychiatrists. They were talking about the efficacy of certain approaches to poverty, addiction, and homelessness. The recidivism percentage was truly appalling. Successful rehabilitation and reentry into society seemed nearly out of reach using the methods they espoused.

When it was my turn to speak, I shared a story to illustrate the power of grassroots healers as they empower their neighbors.

We spent our Easter vacation in San Antonio with the Freddie and Ninfa Garcia at Victory Fellowship. One day, after we'd finished a picnic lunch, Ninfa gave her car keys to three graduates of the program—ex-prostitutes and drug addicts—who had overcome drug addiction. She asked if they'd take my twelve-year-old daughter and two young grandchildren to an amusement park and a movie. They drove off, assuring us they'd be back by 9:00 PM.

I was completely confident, as Ninfa and Freddie were, that our children and grandchildren were in good hands...and they were.

Then I asked the psychiatrists if they would ever have such confidence in their treatments that they would entrust their own children to their clients.

Silence.

Politics as the Enemy of Grace

Black and brown people living in drug-infested, crime-ridden neighborhoods have more in common with whites who live in trailer parks, ride Harleys, and voted for Donald Trump than they have with their elitist overlords.

These groups must come together to speak for themselves, act on their own behalf and form the basis of a new civic and political coalition. They must cease letting the extremists on either side continue to pimp them, and grant each other grace.

It is their children that populate the nation's prisons, foster care system and failing public schools. Their families are being driven out of affordable housing due to gentrification and are victims of drug addiction. Their families suffer from lack of law enforcement when the police are vilified.

Throughout the past four decades, the Woodson Center has created a nationwide network of hundreds of Black, white, and brown grassroots leaders in low-income neighborhoods whose remarkable victories in uplifting their communities and reclaiming lives have built their work on these values and principles.

Getting Personal

One of the first grassroots leaders I met was in South Central Los Angeles, in the middle of the Eastside Crips' gang territory...the most violent you can imagine.

Leon, his wife, and three children were living in a small house right in the center of this neighborhood. Local Black business leaders and homeowners were terrorized by the Eastside Crips daily. They were forced to give money or leave food on their steps daily.

When the gang swept through the streets, Leon had to take his family into the bathroom, the only place they could be safe from drive-by shootings and stray bullets.

Finally, Leon just got tired of it all. He decided to take action, no matter the cost.

He printed wanted posters for the head of the Eastside Crips and posted them with the phone number of a phone booth right outside his house. His neighbors—and the gang members—were absolutely blown away by his courage.

The phone started to ring occasionally. Leon answered with kind words of hope...but no one would "snitch" on the gang's leader. After speaking with more than twenty gang members over a couple of months, he got the call he'd been waiting for. A young man named Quake called and asked Leon to meet in person.

Wide alleys sat behind each house in the neighborhood so that big trash trucks could drive through them. Leon agreed to meet Quake in the alley near his home at exactly five o'clock on that Friday night.

Two cars filled with young men, strapped with automatic weapons and flying their gang colors flew down the alley toward Leon. He put his hands up and walked slowly toward them. Quake stepped out, flashing his gun, and asked Leon what he wanted.

Leon simply said, "I want to talk to you about your life."

Quake waved away the cars and sat on a trash can for three hours, as Leon led him through a Bible study. The next day, Quake brought twenty other gang members to Leon's house to learn more. Within a few months, the Eastside Crips stopped forcing the community to pay "protection" money.

But that wasn't enough for Leon. He called me at the Woodson Center and asked for advice. Together, we decided on a plan to help the gang members direct their time and energy toward something positive: we helped them start a landscaping business.

One night, something miraculous happened. Quake called Leon in the middle of the night to tell him that two men were robbing the neighborhood pharmacy. Leon, Quake, and several other gang members went down to the pharmacy and caught the young men themselves. They called the police together.

The gang who once terrorized this community had become its protectors...living, breathing examples of grace.

Strength Comes from Within

Policymakers on both the left and the right see the poor as hopelessly lost in a sea of pathology with few personal redeeming qualities. They assume that their only hope of rescue will come from the professionals and the intellectual elite. They cannot—will not—recognize the capacities and solutions that exist within America's low-income communities.

For the sake of the poor, we have to overcome our understandable wariness and begin a full and honest conversation about poverty.

We have to understand that neither character alone nor government programs alone are going to solve the problem. We have to understand there are models of reform that do work, if we choose to see them and support them. We have examples of groups that have combined renewed character and supportive private and public generosity that have lifted individuals out of poverty.

Rather than tallying the deficits of low-income communities, I must contend that researchers and analysts should go into those neighborhoods to identify their assets and capacity.

For every percentage of residents in a community exhibiting dysfunction there is a flip-side percentage who have avoided it. We should be asking those people how they did what they did.

Woodson Principles in Action

The Alma Center was created to reach and change the lives of abusive men who have been involved in criminal cases of domestic violence, many of whom have been referred by the justice system.

Rather than focusing on the men's wrongdoing, the program works with its root cause—emotional and physical trauma they had experienced while growing up.

The majority of program participants had a parent who abused drugs or alcohol; half never knew their fathers; many had been victims of sexual and physical abuse. Half had a friend or relative murdered, and more than forty percent had witnessed a homicide.

Through a five-stage program of identifying, dealing with and releasing that pain, participants are empowered to reclaim and renew their lives. That progress is augmented with programs to gain the life skills and job training necessary to secure employment and with a restorative fatherhood program that engenders the compassion, forgiveness, and responsibility necessary to become a caring parent to their children and end the cycle of domestic violence.

The Alma Center and similar groups throughout the nation share a common approach that has resulted in their capacity to reach and salvage lives.

They meet people at their point of need. They don't require their participants to fit into a preconceived definition of "service provision." They offer immediate help where it is most needed and, thereby, establish a bond of trust.

That trust brings hope and vision, the basis of transformation. And that transformation provides a foundation on which practical opportunities for such things as employment, training, and education.

Grace is real, thriving, and delivering action in these neighborhoods!

The Keys to Change

Unheralded community groups and violence-fighting programs hold the key to changing this country. Belief in their effectiveness—a sense of deep optimism—forms the foundation for transformation.

Economic development, education, and other well-meaning programs won't matter unless there's peace in the streets. The peace can only come when predators can be converted to ambassadors of peace. And that's what our grassroots leaders and their organizations do every day. Collectively, they can be an immune system that can be copied throughout this nation…if we truly see them and follow their lead…if we live with an attitude of grace.

Woodson Principle #10

Grace

Love and respect others, even when it's inconvenient. Look at neighborhoods as filled with people who have potential, not dysfunctional victims. The foundation of grace is radical forgiveness; a refusal to be held back by what used to be a hindrance in your life, real or imagined. Be free of bitterness, regret, and uncertainty about the future.

The Challenge and the Change

Maybe it's time we began to recognize the divide in our nation as a war. On the one side are those forces that sow division, discord, and isolation. On the other side, there are forces in society that nurture attachment, connection, and solidarity.

We're witnessing a vast showdown between the "rippers" and "weavers."

The war isn't between one group of good people and another group of bad people. It runs down the middle of every heart. Most of us are part of the problem we complain about.

It's easier to destroy trust than to build it, so the rippers have an advantage. But there are many more weavers, people who yearn to live in loving relationships and trusting communities. The weavers just need what any side in a war needs: training so we know how to wage it, strategies so we know how to win it and a call to arms, so we know why we're in it.

This internal conflict is beginning to define America's future. Partisan debate has become political warfare, and respected opponents have become staunch enemies. Spiritual truth is all but ignored.

Enough is enough.

Woodson Principles in Action

Millions of people currently live in public housing. Thanks to government policies and programs, it has become a billion-dollar industry.

The Woodson Center has identified five specific locations where the residents took over and managed their own projects, organized themselves, took physical control of a public housing project, and employed sanctions and incentives. The result of peers designing solutions for peers has been dramatic.

In the Cochran Gardens project of St. Louis, Missouri, residents rose to action when corpses were found in their elevators. The top four floors of their twelve-story high-rise—some 250 units—had been uninhabitable for more than a dozen years, and crime, vandalism, and drug-related murders filled the community with terror.

The turnaround the residents accomplished when they were allowed to take on management duties won national acclaim, and their dynamic and fearless leader, Bertha Gilkey, was featured on CBS's *60 Minutes*. Sitting on a park bench in a landscaped courtyard, where children played freely and unafraid, she reminded her interviewer that two years earlier he couldn't have walked through that courtyard without the risk of being shot. She declared:

We took failed businesses, turned them around. We took people off welfare in large numbers and put them to work. We took gang members out of gangs and made them husbands and fathers and responsible citizens who now are giving back to the communities, not taking away from them.

We are a neighborhood, not a project. We didn't just fix up the community, we changed the people.

How Will You Respond?

I am convinced that the bondage of that hopelessness and dependency could be broken by giving voice to the Black heritage that was marked by determination, self-sufficiency, and achievement. The truth is that values such as strong families, religion, patriotism, and self-reliance are deeply rooted in authentic Black history.

However, the significant gains of the civil rights movement were built and won by people employing America's founding principles and values, not just protest tactics. Unfortunately, this new group of "civil rights warriors" has all but abandoned these values.

It's time to confront the major impediments to progress in eradicating poverty in our inner cities. The largest roadblocks come from those special interests who graft their agendas on to those of the economically disenfranchised. By perpetrating a victim mentality and poor people's marches that are seldom held without the participation of radical feminists, gay rights activists, environmentalists, and communist apologists who have twisted the plight of the inner-city poor to their own ends.

Worse still, those whose careers or celebrity status rest on the premise that the greatest single obstacle to Black achievement is racism have enforced a gag rule on others who say that self-help and personal responsibility are the keys to progress.

Today's Josephs and pharaohs stand in direct contrast, embodying the founding principles of our nation and the civil rights movement. Neighborhood healers apply the old values of the Black community to a new vision.

They are united in service. They are eager to share ideas and strategies. They offer earnest support to each other in times of struggle and sincerely celebrate one another's victories.

Heroes and Healers

Jack Kemp was an unusual Republican. He came to my office one day and said, "Bob, you have all these leaders here talking about solutions. May I sit in?" For three hours, he sat there and filled a yellow pad full of notes. Afterwards he said, "Bob, I want to help. I want to be a part of this."

Jack used his influence with Steve Bartlett and Dick Armey. They were all freshman in Congress in those days. Jack arranged for other members of Congress to have hearings with my grass-roots leaders in low-income Black public housing projects in Washington, listening to their success stories: how did they drive out the drug leaders; how did they generate small businesses; how did they reduce the costs?

They made headlines all over Washington, because it was so unusual for Republicans to express any concern about welfare and poverty, let alone come into the neighborhoods themselves. Afterward, we wrote seven amendments to the Fair Housing Act.

Jack said, "As members of Congress, Republicans are a minority. But if you can recruit me one Democrat, I'll give you 100 Republican votes."

I recruited my friend from the civil rights movement, Walter Fauntroy, and he agreed to co-sponsor these seven amendments. As a result of Jack's leadership involved with Walter's courage, they passed 430 to zero in the House. In the Senate, they passed ninety-three to zero. They were the first legislation passed with no opposition since we voted to enter World War II...and the last legislation to do so since.

Compassion and Commitment

I believe that when our motivation is duty or even compassion alone, we will often do what is convenient and stop there. In fact, the very notions of "compassion" and "charity" connote a one-way avenue from the gift giver to the receiver.

Getting Personal

When I served as a social worker in the early days, my caseload included a six-year-old girl, Cathy, who as an infant was placed on a farm in the care of an elderly woman. I was absolutely shocked when Cathy's case file contained no indication of an agency site visit during her six years of foster care.

When I met Cathy, I learned she could neither speak nor hear, so I asked how long she had been like that. The foster mother explained that as a baby, Cathy developed a dangerously high fever. The foster mother had called her social worker repeatedly but received no response, so she administered a home remedy.

I took Cathy to a Philadelphia hospital and learned that if her rheumatic fever had simply been treated with antibiotics, she would not have lost her hearing and speech.

My heart broke for her...and she was far from the only child I worked with in similar situations.

When Cathy and I visited the doctor, it was during the Christmas holidays. I took her to see Santa at a downtown department store. I will never forget the joy in her eyes!

I removed Cathy from the isolated farm and placed her with a family with four foster children who enrolled her in the Pennsylvania School for the Deaf. Had I the means, I would have adopted her myself.

The Challenge and the Change

Let me leave you with a strong challenge:

Changing policy takes determination, because there will be opposition.

Changing policy takes guts, because it will challenge powerful interests.

Changing neighborhoods takes compassion, because you will have to change your attitude.

Changing culture takes strong character, because it requires long-term commitment.

Changing lives takes determination, grit, and grace, because you are dealing with decades of suffering and obstacles.

Will you dive in with me, and bring the change?

EPILOGUE

By Alicia Manning
Senior Program Director, Bradley Foundation

Just over 20 years ago, I met a man who would turn my world upside down. You see, I've dedicated my life to helping those who struggle with poverty, addiction, mental illness, lack of education, or other difficult needs.

I began working with the Bradley Foundation, and in 1998 my boss, William Schambra, introduced me to Bob Woodson. Bob had built quite a reputation on Capitol Hill and in the human services arena, not just because of his successful influence on welfare reform legislation, but because his unique solutions worked.

Since then, the Woodson Center has been the single most influential organization in the work of the Lynde and Harry Bradley Foundation. In the first several years of its giving (beginning in 1986), the Foundation made very conventional local grants, largely benefiting established institutions of higher education, hospitals, and conventional social services organizations.

Then Bob offered his time and expertise, teaching us to look instead for people who are authentically working as agents of change in their own communities. Frankly, this is the opposite of standard approach, where non profits and government organizations bring in outside "experts" to address societal problems. Unfortunately, when these "outsiders" leave, the communities often return to their previous states of poverty and crime quickly.

But Bob's strategy and practice of empowering people to make a difference in their own communities brings about lasting change for two simple reasons. One, these agents of change live, work, and love their neighbors and neighborhoods. They are already embedded in the community and will stay long-term. Second, community leaders know the needs. The real needs, not the ones that far away experts assume are there.

Working with Bob brought me into contact with hundreds of community-shapers, agents of change, and committed partners. I learned to look for evidence of places where people are already helping their neighbors, pouring into their lives, and bringing about lasting transformation.

Over the last twenty-odd years, the Bradley Foundation has awarded philanthropic support according to Bob Woodson's principles, and his team has continued to offer advice, support, and immersion in a community of like-minded people. As a result of this longstanding partnership, the Bradley Foundation has made more than $100 million in grants to grassroots and faith-based groups offering community-based, self-help-oriented solutions that effectively address social issues others regard as intractable.

We have also continued to partner with the Woodson Center to elevate the work of credible, creative leaders like Victor, who are morally compelled to solve problems with which they are familiar.

In fact, when Bob introduced me to Victor, he was working as a substitute teacher and night guard "to support his community outreach habit." He started a small youth basketball team out of his truck, hoping to give the kids in his neighborhood an alternative to gang membership.

They played so well in their first year that they were invited to a national tournament in Florida. Victor couldn't pay for his team to travel, so he contacted me. The Bradley Foundation provided a $5,000 grant for their trip.

Today, Running Rebels is a $5 million organization, fielding teams in inner-city neighborhoods all over the country. Coaches invest their lives in these kids, and I wish you could hear all of their stories. Thousands of kids have grown up into strong men and women with deep community roots and solid family values.

In the world of foundations and funding, it's easy to become deeply cynical. Leading with money rarely results in lasting change. Outsider intervention fails. Non-profits struggle to deliver on their promises. Even government organizations come and go.

That's why we have directed countless people—both practitioners and other funders—to seek Bob's wisdom and guidance about how to conduct, identify, and evaluate transformational work amidst a nonprofit culture that values the transactional because it is easier to enumerate.

I remember Bob's first words to me so clearly: *"Find the people who are utterly driven by the problem they know they can solve. Find the ones who can't sleep at night because of how committed they are; the ones who are available at all hours of the night to those they serve. They can't stop loving people…and neither can we."*

ACKNOWLEDGMENTS

One of the most difficult chores in writing a book is trying to appropriately recognize everyone who contributed to its successful completion. I pray anyone I neglect to mention will understand it as an oversight, not a lack of affection or appreciation on my part.

None of this would be possible without the heroic patience, grace, and unfailing support of my wife, Ellen. Few decisions will test a marriage more than telling your spouse you are leaving the security of an established think tank to start a new nonprofit at a time when many are closing their doors. But one such decision followed shortly thereafter when I invited a gang leader involved in an ongoing Washington, DC turf war to come live with our family. After a short silence, Ellen consented, and within hours she and Wayne were baking together in the kitchen. For forty-three years we have walked together, sharing every joy and sorrow. Greatest among the joys are our children Jamal and Tanya and our grandchildren, Arianna, Robert III, Cianne, and our newest addition, Raymond Roberto Monestel. Gone but never forgotten is our son, Rob.

My appreciation also goes out to my extended family, those members of the Woodson Center staff who have labored with me for more than twenty years. Stephanie Detrio, my director of finance, Collette Caprara, editor and writer, Curtis Watkins, director of constituent mobilization, Hattie Porterfield, my executive assistant, Phyllis Stukes, and—last but certainly not least—my chief operating officer, Terence Mathis. I can think of no one who has influenced my life more than this man, who is wise beyond his years, a meticulous manager, and faithful to everyone we serve. A prospective supporter once asked me who in the organization could tell me I was wrong, and my immediate answer was Terence. His spirited challenges have served as guard rails that have kept us faithful to our mission. Although he has moved on to the next phase of his professional life, as many of us say, "Goodbye ain't always gone."

I am indebted to my circle of intellectual advisors who keep me abreast of developments in the policy and academic worlds, chief among them Bill Schambra. Alicia Manning, of the Bradley Foundation, is carrying this knowledge to the next generation. I am deeply grateful to all our financial supporters, who are too many to name, but I want to especially acknowledge those who invested in us from the beginning, including the Lynde and Harry Bradley Foundation, the Sarah Schiff Foundation, Achilles and Bodman, John M. Olin, and many others.

Lastly, I want to thank the grassroots leaders I have been blessed to serve all of my adult life, whose work gives meaning and value to everything I do. Brother Carl Hardrick, who is affectionally referred to as "the mayor of the ghetto" in Hartford, Connecticut, as well as Andrew Woods, Willie Peterson, Gary and Pat Wyatt, Paul and Cindy Grodell, Marva Mitchell, Tyrone Parker, Jubal Garcia, Sarah Attica, and many others. In all of the years we have gathered at meetings, retreats, and conferences, racial conflict never reared its head. We were united to overcome the brokenness in our lives and focus on redemption and transformation. I pray everyone reading this book can experience what that kind of gathering is like.

Many of my closest friends and allies have letters in front of their names not behind them: they are an "Ex" something, rather than a "Ph.D." in something. But I have found their expertise to be far more valuable to the betterment of humanity. Among this group are my adopted sons, the ex-gang members who became ambassadors of peace in the Benning Terrace Public Housing complex. When our son Robert, Jr. died in a tragic accident eighteen years ago, all of these young men came to the memorial service and surrounded my family and me with love and support. They gave me the strength to go on, reminding me that I had eighteen others sons who needed me. At a time when the tidal wave of grief was so overwhelming that I contemplated taking my own life, their love saved me.